ScrapMania

More Quick-Pieced Scrap Quilts

Sally Schneider

That Patchwork Place®

Credits

Editor-in-Chief . . . . Barbara Weiland
Technical Editor . . . . Laura M. Reinstatler
Managing Editor . . . . Greg Sharp
Copy Editor . . . . Liz McGehee
Proofreader . . . . Tina Cook
Text and Cover Design . . . . Joanne Lauterjung
Typesetting . . . . Joanne Lauterjung
Sandra Seligmiller
Photography . . . . Brent Kane
Illustration and Graphics . . . . Laurel Strand

Scrapmania ©
© 1994 by Sally Schneider
That Patchwork Place, Inc., PO Box 118, Bothell, WA 98041-0118
USA

Printed in the United States of America
99 98 97 96 95 94   6 5 4 3 2

Dedication

To my mother, Betty Bax George, who taught me to sew. Her gift of a handmade pillow was also a gift of inspiration and direction—an invitation to match her talent and accomplishment, and a direction for my own creative urges.

Acknowledgments

The following people have helped make this book possible. I am indebted to them for their help and support. Thanks go to:

My students, who loved scrap quilts so much they wanted more;

Mary Kelleher, who listened while I chatted on the chair lift;

Sue Linker, Judy Sogn, Nancy Koorenny, Cheri Potts, Sally Broeker, and Jenny Resch for all kinds of help;

Nancy Koorenny, Kari Lane, Barb Eikmeier, and Carol Anfinson, who helped out with their wonderful quilting;

Barb Eikmeier, Maureen McGee, Sally Ambrose, Pam Montgomery, Margie Fisher, Bee Molmen, Tami Josties, Linda Gabrielse, Lynn Styczynsky, Nancy Martin, Dana Masera, Lu Storm, and Marnie Allard, who made quilts;

The staff at That Patchwork Place for their support and encouragement;

Marion Shelton for her support through three books;

My sons, David, Drew, and Ted, who make me proud;

And especially to my friend Judy Kowalsky, who has helped me through some hard times.

Thank you all.

Library of Congress Cataloging-in-Publication Data

Schneider, Sally.
        Scrapmania / Sally Schneider.
            p. cm.
            ISBN 1-56477-050-8 :
            1. Patchwork—Patterns. 2. Quilting—Patterns.
        I. Title
        TT835.S348 1994
        746.9'7—dc20   94-3126
                                                                                   CIP

Contents

Preface

Scrap quilts have been my special love for a long time, and I keep trying to find new ways to adapt traditional patterns for scraps. My other love is finding easier ways to make quilts without sacrificing accuracy or beauty. This book includes two new techniques that I have developed, both quite by accident: no-mark folded corners and Mary's Triangles.

In 1985, while on a ski trip with some friends, it occurred to me that a Shaded Four Patch, a unit that quilters use a great deal, was difficult to construct. It involved several bias seams as well as individually cut pieces. The quick-piecing technique used for quarter-square triangles provided the needed clue for streamlining the Four Patch unit's construction. I called my technique "Mary's Triangles" be-

cause when the solution to the problem presented itself (like a bolt of lightning out of nowhere), I was sitting on a chair lift with my friend Mary. She patiently listened to me describe the problem and its solution, then watched as I drew it in the snow. Mary is not a quilter, but she listened to me jabber away and tried to understand what I was explaining. What more could you ask of a friend, except that she ski at the same pace you do? (Mary does!)

Since that time, I have worked a great deal with Mary's Triangles. I am excited to present the technique in this book, along with six different ways to use it. The variations are almost endless; my inspiration on that chair lift may be just what you need to spark your imagination and to make wonderful new scrap quilts.

Introduction

Can you remember when and why you were first interested in quiltmaking? For many, quiltmaking is a natural progression from sewing clothing. After finishing the clothes, you have all those scraps left, and heaven forbid that you throw them away! You have to find something to do with these pieces, and quilts are the most obvious solution—scrap quilts.

The scrap quilt on my bed, made of leftover pieces from my mother's drapery business, was my first introduction to quilts. Maybe you grew up with scrap quilts on all the beds, too, looking at all the little fabric pieces that you remembered as dresses, aprons, or kitchen curtains.

When it comes time for us to make quilts, we don't all necessarily make scrap quilts as our first attempt, but most of us have a connection to scrap quilts in our earliest quilting background.

As you contemplate your quilting experience, think about your fabric collection. Every quilter I have ever met has been a fabric collector. The more interested you become in quilting, the more important fabric becomes, and the larger your collection grows. As the scraps accumulate, you try to imagine what to do with all this fabric. The obvious answer? Scrap quilts! At some time in your quilting career, if it hasn't happened already, you will become convinced that scrap quilts are the answer to the fabric collection question.

Since the publication of my first book, *Scrap Happy*, several years ago, I have become even more enamored of scrap quilts. Because I am a die-hard quick piecer, I have continued to cut strips and make half-square triangles for scrap quilts as described in that book. Eventually, boxes of strips and half-square triangle units threatened to overrun my entire sewing room. It became apparent that it was time to find more uses for these units.

I have always loved traditional patterns and quickly realized that, although many of these patterns were usually made in just a few colors, they could also be made as successful scrap quilts if the principles of value distribution were followed. A discussion of the importance of value begins on page 7.

Fabric

I have been making quilts since 1972 and have been collecting fabric for almost as long. My collection has grown from a small box of donated scraps to a small dresser, then a second dresser, and now it completely fills a ten-by-eight-foot closet. (Those are just the prints; there is another cabinet for solids, and another whole closet for clothing fabric.) Fabric is packed tightly in this closet from wall to wall, floor to ceiling. Stacks of new fabric are piled on the floor, waiting for a place to open up (kind of like the parking lot at the mall at Christmastime). I have threatened to hold a garage sale to get rid of the older stuff, but when I look at the fabric and remember buying it (as you probably remember where you bought every piece), I find myself unwilling to part with it; I need to put it into a quilt.

Traveling around the country teaching quiltmaking, I always end up in at least one quilt shop per city. I always buy something, since I feel it is my duty to support every one of these shops. Sometimes it's just a few fat quarters, but my collection keeps growing, and I am tempted to build an addition to the house just to store my fabric.

Purchasing Fabric

When purchasing fabric, follow several guidelines. The first and most important is, buy what you love. Fabric that you do not find particularly appealing will remain in the closet. There will always be a reason not to choose this piece of fabric, and it will take up space (and budget) better used for another purpose.

Try to find fabrics you love in all color families, remembering that variety is the spice of scrap quilts, as well as it is of life. For many years I disliked the color orange but recently found some orange fabrics that are appealing. I purchased small amounts of these fabrics and used them in some of the scrap quilts, and I like the results. My mother always told me that red and yellow are important to scrap quilts. She was right—those two colors add sparkle to my quilts.

Don't be afraid of unusual fabrics. Plaids, large prints, geometric styles, and conversation prints with identifiable items on them all add interest to scrap quilts. The "Interweave" quilt on page 22 even includes a square of fabric with the logo of my family's beloved Denver Broncos (difficult to explain since we live in Seattle Seahawk territory)!

I usually purchase ½- to 1-yard pieces, depending upon how much I love the fabric. I also purchase fat quarters (18" x 22" fabric pieces), particularly in combinations selected by people with a much better color sense than mine. For something that might make a nice border, I purchase 2 yards, and when I see a good background fabric, I usually buy 5 yards.

Don't ever apologize for liking one specific color combination. Ignore people who tell you that you make too many red-and-blue quilts. You are pursuing an activity that gives you pleasure, so use fabrics and colors that you enjoy and make you feel happy. When the time is right to try something different, you will know it. (Remember, I'm buying orange now.) Give yourself permission to experiment, to make something perhaps less successful than you might like the first time or two. You will become more comfortable with something new in the process. Do whatever you must do to keep quiltmaking the pleasurable activity that made you pursue it in the first place!

Combining Fabrics for Scrap Quilts

While teaching "Scrap Happy Quilts," I discovered that people are sometimes intimidated by the idea of using fabrics that don't "match." To help these people stretch beyond their comfort zone, I have adopted several scrap-quilt techniques that allow quilters to gradually broaden their abilities to combine fabrics.

The first method is to use a traditional block design and make each block with a pleasing fabric combination, using a common background fabric. (No two blocks should have the same fabric except this background piece.) After putting these blocks together with sashing strips, you have a lovely scrap quilt, allowing you to see that many fabrics can be successfully combined in the same quilt. "Wyoming Valley Star" on page 23 is an example of this method.

The second method is to use a fabric "menu," where each part of a block is a particular color, but many different fabrics of that color are used. This provides a cohesive visual design while allowing a large variety of fabrics to be used. Barb Eikmeier's "Burgoyne Surrounded" on page 19 was made using this method.

The third method is the most difficult for many people. Here, random colors and fabrics are used haphazardly throughout the quilt. Dark-value fabrics are used where the design requires dark, and light-value fabrics are used where the design requires light, but there is no rhyme or reason to the color, pattern, or compatibility of the fabrics. See "Interweave" on page 22 for an example. These are my favorite quilts to make. I can abandon all the principles of color matching that I learned long ago!

Value

No element is more important to the design of a scrap quilt than value. Value refers to a color's degree of lightness or darkness. A pale color is called a light value, and a dark color is called a dark value. If you know what value is and how to use it, you can make successful scrap quilts every time. The concept of value must be learned and practiced.

To a quilter, value means only how dark or light a fabric is compared to the fabrics around it. This comparison is crucial to the assignment of value. To determine value in a group of fabrics, separate them into three groups. (I use no more than three values in my quilts, and usually only two: dark and light.) Place the darkest fabrics in one group, the lightest fabrics in a second group, and the medium fabrics in a third group. Squint at these fabric groups, making sure there is nothing in the medium group darker than in the dark group or lighter than in the light group.

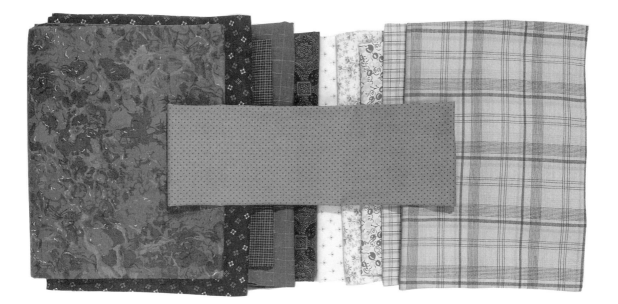

Scrap Preparation

Adapting quick-piecing techniques for the construction of scrap quilts requires some advance planning and preparation—in other words, a system. After examining a great many traditional quilt patterns, I realized that most of the designs had several units in common, for example, various-size squares and half-square triangle units. By preparing specific common sizes of these units ahead of time (preferably before I put the fabric away on the shelves) and storing them by size, I would be ready to start construction of a scrap quilt, using a traditional pattern, without having to cut all those fabrics before I started sewing. I found that the most useful pieces to prepare were 1½", 2", and 2½" strips, and half-square triangle units cut 2½", 3", and 3½" to finish 2", 2½", and 3". You will also find 5½" strips very useful to have on hand for the quilts in this book that use Mary's Triangles techniques.

I cut fat quarters ahead of time into these units as shown above right. While the strips are only 22" long, they are sufficient to make a scrap quilt. By saving the cutaway triangles left from constructing folded corners in other projects (see "Folded Corners," page 13), I can stockpile the 2" finished half-square triangle units required for some of the quilts. When using a 3½" x 3½" fabric square for folded corners, you can trim the left-over half-square triangle unit to 2½", yielding a 2" finished unit.

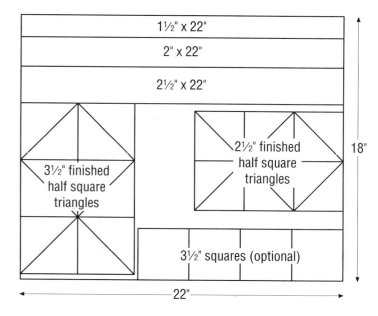

Many of the patterns in this book suggest using fat eighths as scrap sources. Although these 9" x 22" pieces are smaller, they offer double the variety for the price of fat quarters.

Some of the quilts in this book yield leftover 2" finished half-square triangle units; several of the patterns require them. I have begun saving these pieces and have also begun making them to have on hand.

Tools

Scrap quilts require the same tools as used for any quiltmaking endeavor.

Rulers: It is most important have a 6" x 24" acrylic ruler marked in ⅛" increments. Other favorites include 6" and 15" squares.

Cutting tools: A rotary cutter with a large blade is indispensable for making quick-pieced quilts. Make sure the blade is very sharp; replace it when cutting becomes difficult.

Cutting mat: You will need one to protect the table or work area and to prolong the life of the blade. I like a translucent one made by Charvoz because I can see all colors of fabric on it. If this is not available, a board that is green on one side and white on the other is a good substitute. This way, you have two cutting backgrounds to choose from.

Scissors: Use a small pair to clip threads and trim seams. They must be very sharp and must cut evenly all the way to the point.

Marking tools: I use a regular #2 pencil or a colored pencil for dark fabrics. For a sharp line that doesn't distort or pull the fabric, keep the point very sharp and hold the pencil almost parallel to the fabric.

Needles: Use size 80 European or size 12 U.S. needles. Change the needle often, after every 4–6 hours of actual sewing time.

Thread: 100% cotton thread is best for sewing quilts; test a few different brands to see what works best for you. I use off-white when sewing light colors and gray when sewing darker colors.

Masking tape: Buy a roll of ¼"-wide tape for marking quilting lines and one of ¾"-wide (the stuff that goes on sale at the hardware store) for marking quilting lines and stitching lines on the sewing machine.

Adhesive seam gauge: I like to use Sew Perfect. This product, available in quilt shops, is about ¾" x 4½" and ⅛" thick. It is sticky on one side and has a pretty fabric on the other side. I cut this into 6 pieces, each ⅜" x 1½", and use it to mark a ¼"-wide seam allowance on my sewing machine. (See "Accurate Seam Allowances" on pages 10–11.)

Reducing glass: I frequently use a door peephole (available at hardware stores) to look at groups of fabric to determine a good value distribution. Looking at the fabrics through the wrong end of a pair of binoculars makes the fabric colors recede, revealing them only as darks and lights. It is easy to see if something stands out or is in the wrong place. I prefer to squint my eyes for the first evaluation of value distribution, then use the peephole as a final check.

General Directions

Accurate Seam Allowances

Rulers can be a source of inaccuracy in sewing. Some are not printed straight. Make sure that the ¼" mark is the same on both sides and both ends of the ruler and use the same ruler for the entire quilt.

Because most of the pieces used for the scrap quilts in this book are cut to a specific measurement, including precise ¼"-wide seams, you must be able to stitch this seam allowance consistently and accurately so that all the pieces fit together.

Follow the diagrams and instructions below to mark the correct ¼"-wide seam allowance on your machine.

With the presser foot in the up position, place the ruler on your sewing machine. Align the ruler's ¼" line with the sewing machine needle. Lower the needle slowly until it touches the ¼" line. Lower the presser foot to help keep the ruler in position.

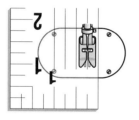

Align the ruler with another mark or line somewhere on the sewing machine to be sure that the line you draw is straight.

Using a permanent marker with a fine point, draw a line along the ruler's edge. This line will be the temporary seam allowance.

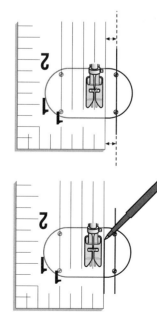

Test the seam allowance in the following manner. Cut three 2"-wide strips of 100% cotton scrap fabrics. They should be about 6" long. Stitch the three strips together using the seam-allowance guide you marked. Press the seams to one side; measure the width. It should be exactly 5".

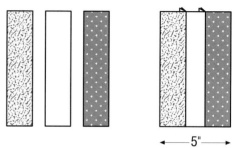

If it is not, adjust the guideline and sew strips together, repeating until it is correct. (The guide marks come off with alcohol if you need to remove them.)

Use the permanent marker to draw a sewing guide in the correct place. I have a piece of masking tape on the throat plate of my machine with all the appropriate lines marked on it. This tape stays there permanently, so that I can place a stitching guide on the appropriate line and then remove it when it's no longer needed. The tape "master" allows me to keep a permanent record of the proper measurement lines.

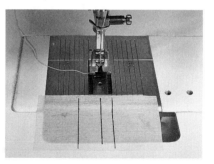

When machine piecing with a ¼"-wide seam allowance, it is helpful to have more than just a line to guide the fabric. A ridge of layered masking tape, moleskin, or my favorite, Sew Perfect, are all suitable alternatives. Place the stitching guide on the throat plate in front of the feed dog as shown. It is easy to line up the fabric layers and keep them straight using this guide, and the ridge won't interfere with pins.

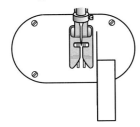

Whatever material you use to form this ridge, be careful not to let it get under the presser foot, as this would prevent the foot from feeding the fabric at an even pressure as it is drawn under the needle. The fabric does not feed straight if the presser foot is impeded.

Pressing

When pressing any patchwork, I use steam. Many references suggest avoiding it, claiming that steam stretches the fabric. I believe pulling on the edges while pressing, not the steam, stretches the fabric.

When pressing strips, lay them on the ironing board with the darker strip on top (or the strip toward which you want to press the seam). Press the seam flat first, in the closed position, to set the stitches and remove any puckers caused by the stitching.

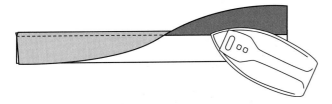

Then use the iron to push the top layer of fabric away from the bottom one in the strip unit. Don't pull the fabric back with your hand.

Press one row of a multilayered strip-pieced unit at a time; repeat the above steps for each row.

Press half-square triangle units using the same principle. Place the units on the ironing board with the darker side on top (or the side toward which you want to press the seam allowance). Carefully lift the tip of the triangle with your fingers—the iron is hot! Then, let the side of the iron gently push the top triangle away.

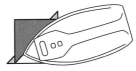

Some quilts require the folded-corner technique shown on page 13. Treat these in the same way as half-square triangle units.

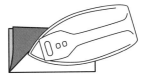

When pressing all these units, remember that the key is to press, not iron. Let the side of the iron gently push the piece into place, then place the iron on top of the seam and press down. Don't push the iron back and forth or push the tip of the iron into the seam. It might catch on the seam and stretch the piece.

Strip Piecing

Quilt designs composed of only squares and rectangles can be made quickly and accurately by cutting strips a specific width and sewing them together in a specific order. These strips are then called a set of strata or a strip-pieced unit. The next step is to cut the strip-pieced unit apart into the required pieces and combine them with other pieces made in the same manner.

CUTTING STRIPS

To cut with the rotary cutter, push it away from you along the edge of the ruler, using a smooth motion and consistent pressure. Begin with the blade on the cutting mat about 1" in front of the edge of the fabric. If the blade does not cut through all layers, press a little harder.

With experience, it will become apparent how much pressure to use.

Before cutting strips, it is essential to straighten the edge of the fabric. Fold the pressed fabric in half, matching the selvages.

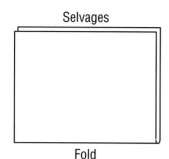

Selvages

Fold

Fold the fabric again, lining up the fold of the fabric with the selvages. You now have four layers of fabric.

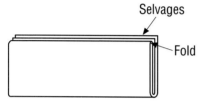

Selvages

Fold

Align a square ruler along the folded edge of the fabric (opposite the selvages). Slide the ruler toward the raw edge on the left side of the fabric until it is as close to the edge as possible, with all four layers of fabric still underneath it. Push a larger ruler against the small one; remove the small ruler and cut against the larger ruler. (If you are left-handed, reverse the tool positions.)

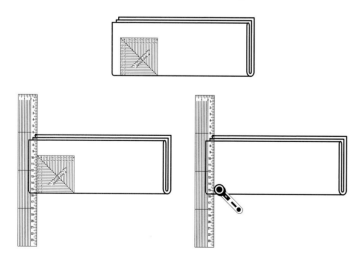

Cut off the uneven edge of fabric. Discard the trimmings. Align the newly cut straight edges un-der the ruler's vertical line indicating the desired strip width. Cut strips as needed.

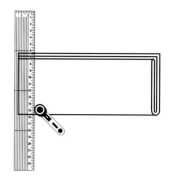

Strip-Pieced Unit Construction

Sew strips together in the order required for your design. Using a hot iron with steam, press the seam allowances toward the darker fabric unless otherwise directed.

Using the seam lines as the horizontal guide for the ruler, trim the ends of the strip-pieced unit to remove the selvages.

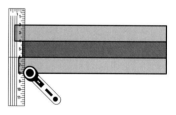

Cut rectangles from the strip-pieced unit us-ing the width specified in your directions.

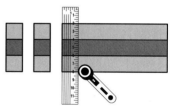

You can usually cut across two or three strip-pieced units at one time, but any more tend to slip out of position resulting in inaccurate cuts.

To sew rectangles together, match the inter-secting seam lines, with seam allowances lying in opposite directions. Pin intersections on either side of the seam, through the seam allowances.

When matching triangle points, keep the point you are matching on top so you can see an intersection of seams on the wrong side of the squares. It looks like a Y.

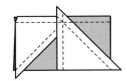

Be sure to sew exactly through the intersection of the seams so that the point is not cut off.

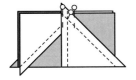

If you must match a point to a point, as in eight-point centers, push a pin directly through both points and pull it snug. Place a pin to either side of the first pin, through the seam allowances, and remove the first pin. Stitch through the intersection of the seams.

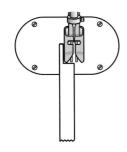

Press seams as you sew them, being careful not to stretch or otherwise distort bias edges.

Folded Corners

This is a quick and accurate way to add a triangle corner to a square or rectangle without cutting triangles. You start with a large square and a small square.

1. Place a piece of masking tape on your machine straight from the needle toward you. Trim it away from the feed dog.

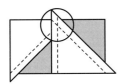

2. Place the small square on top of the large square in one corner and begin stitching exactly in the corner of the top square. As you stitch, keep the opposite corner directly on the edge of the masking tape so you can sew a straight line without having to draw it first on the fabric.

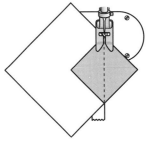

Note:

To avoid wasting the cutaway corners that result with this technique, draw a line ½" to the left of the needle on your sewing machine. (You may need another piece of masking tape to the left of your feed dog.) Line up the sewn seam with the new ½" line and sew again. Cut between the stitched lines to yield one unit with a folded corner and a half-square triangle unit to save for another project. (Using a 3½" top square yields a 2" finished half-square triangle unit. It must be trimmed to size.)

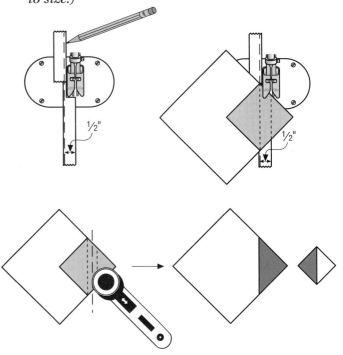

Half-Square Triangle Units

To quickly produce a large quantity of squares consisting of two right-angle triangles, use the grid system described below. It is fast and accurate. This method requires two pieces of fabric of the same size placed right sides together, a ruler with a grid marked in ⅛" increments, and a very sharp pencil or other marking implement. Mechanical pencils and black fine-point, ball-point pens work well for marking, as do silver, white, or yellow colored pencils, providing you keep their points sharp.

The size of the grid squares is determined by adding ⅞" to the required finished size of the half-square triangle unit. For example, if you need a half-square triangle unit that finishes to 2", the squares must measure 2⅞".

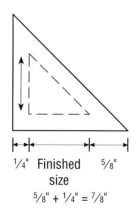

¼"   Finished   ⅝"
        size
⅝" + ¼" = ⅞"

This requires a ¼"-wide seam allowance on all sides of the triangle, but if your presser foot is not exactly ¼" wide, don't despair. You can make a marking guide to compensate for that difference. Refer to "Marking Guides" on pages 16–17.

Use the finished-size measurement plus ⅞" (or your specially constructed marking guide) for the grid size.

1. Begin by drawing a grid of squares on the back of the lightest or easiest-to-mark fabric. To save fabric, orient your grids with the longest side of the grid parallel to the crosswise grain of the fabric. Draw a horizontal line on the fabric close to the edge, then measure the required distance from this line and draw another line. Repeat to the end of the fabric.

Crosswise grain

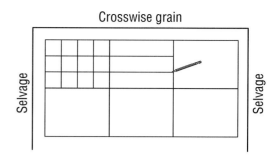

Selvage   Selvage

2. Line up a horizontal line on the ruler with one of the lines you have drawn to determine an exact 90° angle. With the ruler near the edge of the fabric, draw a vertical line. Measure the required distance from this line and draw another line. Repeat to the end of the fabric to resemble the lines of a checkerboard.

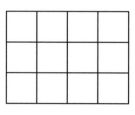

𝒩ote:

For ease of sewing and for the sake of accuracy, the grid should be no larger than three squares by four squares, for a total of twelve squares. This will yield twenty-four half-square triangle units.

3. Draw a diagonal line in every other row of squares in one direction, then every other row of squares in the other direction as shown.

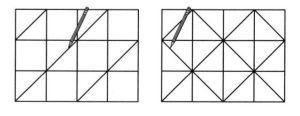

𝒩ote:

The grid should have one diagonal line in each square. If a square has an X through it, it is incorrect and you must redraw your lines. Look at the diagonal lines carefully. You should be able to trace a continuous line through the entire grid without lifting your pencil and sew a continuous line without cutting your thread.

4. To help keep the two pieces of fabric from slipping, press them before you begin sewing, or pin if you wish.

5. Begin sewing in a corner, placing the edge of the presser foot on the drawn line and sewing straight to the end of the line. Put the needle in the down position and rotate the fabric 90°, then continue sewing to the next corner. Rotate again and sew. Keep rotating 90° and sewing straight lines until you reach the end.

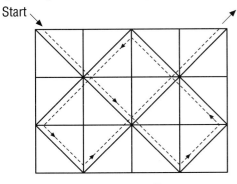

Grid sewn halfway

6. Now rotate the fabric 180° and sew back to the start, being sure to keep the edge of the presser foot on the drawn line. When finished, every diagonal line should have a sewn line on each side.

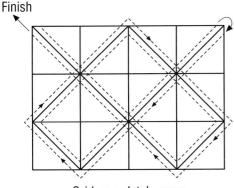

Grid completely sewn

If you need fewer half-square triangle units, sew a half grid. It looks like this and yields twelve half-square triangle units.

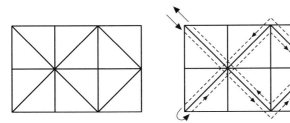

7. Cut the grid apart exactly on each drawn line, yielding two already-sewn half-square triangle units for each drawn square of the grid.

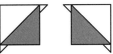

8. Press the seams toward the darker side, unless the directions for the specific quilt you are making instruct differently. To reduce bulk, trim off the little triangles sticking out beyond the square on two corners, after you have pressed the seams.

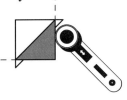

Quarter-Square Triangle Units

Quick-pieced triangles can be used as the basis for more than just squares made with two right-angle triangles. By changing the size of the grid, you can easily make squares with four right-angle triangles. For all the following designs, the grid should be 1¼" larger than the desired finished size of the square. If you cannot use the right-hand edge of your presser foot as a guide for stitching a ¼"-wide seam, see "Marking Guides" on pages 16–17.

Place two half-square triangle units right sides together. Match seam lines and draw a diagonal line through the square, crossing the seam line as shown. Stitch ¼" from the diagonal line on both sides. Cut on the line to create the two quarter-square triangle units.

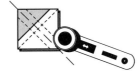

Use two colors to make these squares.

Use three colors to make these squares.

Use four colors to make these squares.

Marking Guides

If you cannot use the edge of your presser foot for a ¼" stitching guide, you must make adjustments for the variation when measuring grids for quick-pieced triangles. By making your own measuring tool, you will be able to draw a grid tailor-made to your required triangle size and to your machine's presser foot.

The marking guide resembles a cutting ruler but is constructed from heavy template plastic or heavy poster board. Use it to draw the grid only, *not* as a cutting guide. Remember, you will need a different marking guide for each size triangle you want to make.

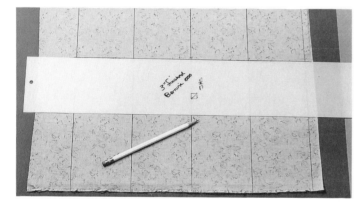

To measure for the marking guide:

If you don't understand how this technique works after reading through the instructions, don't worry. It works, but to understand it you must do it. Just complete each of the steps below.

1. Draw a square of the required finished size on a sheet of paper. Do not use graph paper. Use the ruler you normally use to cut strips. Be sure the square is as precise as you can possibly make it. Draw a diagonal line through the square. Extend the line about 1" each way.

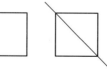

2. Remove the thread from your sewing machine and place the right edge of the presser foot on this diagonal line. Stitch a line parallel to the drawn line on the paper.

Sew on one side of the line.

3. With your ruler, add ¼"-wide seam allowances to the two adjacent sides of the square opposite the sewn diagonal line. Extend these seam allowances to the sewn line.

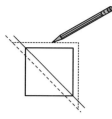

4. Measure from the ¼"-wide seam allowance line at the top of the square to the intersection of the sewn line and the ¼"-wide seam-allowance line. Use this measurement to make a marking guide for quick-pieced triangles of this size on your machine. (See directions below.)

Measure here to determine the width of your marking guide.

This method will also work for squares made of four triangles. Draw a square of the required finished size as you did above, but this time draw diagonal lines both ways through the square. Add the ¼"-wide seam allowance to the right of the square.

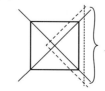

With the edge of the presser foot on the diagonal line, sew parallel to both diagonal lines and measure the distance between the intersections of the sewn lines and the ¼"-wide seam-allowance line to determine the size of your marking guide.

Measure here to determine the width of your marking guide.

To make the marking guide:

1. Measure the required distance as calculated above and mark this measurement on template plastic.

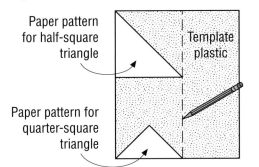

Paper pattern for half-square triangle

Template plastic

Paper pattern for quarter-square triangle

2. Place an acrylic ruler on the plastic, making sure all vertical lines are parallel, and score the plastic lightly with an old rotary-cutter blade. Occasionally, the ruler may slip on the template plastic; to prevent this, place small rubber circles or pieces of rubber band between the plastic and the ruler.

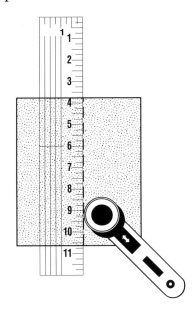

3. Bend the plastic until it snaps on the scored line.
4. After you have made your marking guide, check to see that it is accurate and that the measurements on both ends are the same.
5. For quick reference, write the size of the half-square triangle unit on the marking guide.
6. To mark the grid for quick-pieced triangles onto your fabric, use the marking guide in place of a ruler. (See pages 14–15.)
7. Make a half grid of half-square triangle units to test the guide. The half-square triangle units should be ½" larger than the size of the square you started with.

Gallery of Quilts

For My Dad by Sally Schneider, 1992, Puyallup, Washington, 54" x 61". The Catherine Wheels pattern used here was seen on an antique quilt owned by Cathy Hansen. It was made as a Christmas gift for my father. Collection of William George. Directions on page 32.

Fantasy Fireworks by Dana Masera, 1993, Bremerton, Washington, 56" x 64". This Catherine Wheels quilt has wonderful fireworks quilted in gold in the border. Directions on page 32.

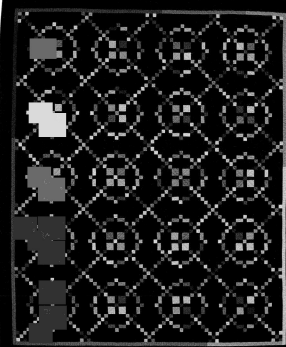

Burgoyne Surrounded by Maureen McGee, 1993, Lansing, Kansas, 83" x 100". Dramatic use of a black background with light solids gives this traditional favorite a different look. Directions on page 35.

Burgoyne Surrounded by Sally Schneider, 1993, Puyallup, Washington, 46" x 64". Using one common background fabric with the scraps emphasizes the circular pattern. Directions on page 35.

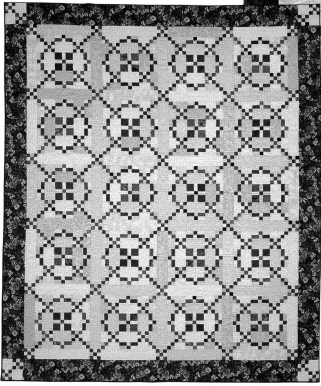

Burgoyne Surrounded by Barbara Eikmeier, 1993, Ft. Irwin, California, 85" x 101". The many background fabrics and the "fabric menu" of teal and fuchsia give this Burgoyne Surrounded yet another look. Directions on page 35.

Friendship Star by Sally Schneider, 1993, Puyallup, Washington, 72" x 88". Sally collected squares from students and fellow guild members for more than a year before she made this quilt. The variety of background fabrics weaves a rich tapestry. Directions on page 40.

Friends of Marion by Sally Schneider, 1993, Puyallup, Washington, 52" x 37". This friendship quilt was made for Marion Shelton, Acquisitions Administrative Assistant at That Patchwork Place. Many of the authors who have written for That Patchwork Place signed the background blocks. Collection of Marion Shelton. Directions on page 40.

Great Denver Barter by Pam Montgomery, 1993, Denver, Colorado, 87" x 103". The off-center Log Cabin design gives the illusion of curves with only straight seams. Pam traded this quilt for a new kitchen floor, thus the title. Collection of Jeff Kruck. Directions on page 43.

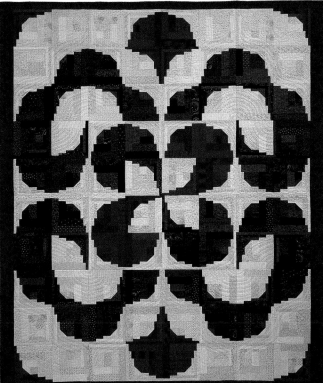

Suzie's Sun Ring by Pam Montgomery, 1993, Denver, Colorado, 47" x 47". Concentric, lobed circles of light and dark are formed with this Log Cabin variation. Collection of Paul and Mary Rosier. Directions on page 43.

Ladybug, Ladybug, I Can't Fly Away Home
by Linn Styczenski, 1993, Grosse Pointe Park, Michigan, 54" x 73".
Linn's quilt became a farewell to her home in Grand Rapids.
Ladybug buttons adorn some of the blocks, and friends from her
old home signed some of the squares. Directions on page 48.

Interweave by Sally Schneider, 1993, Puyallup, Washington,
70" x 90". The arrangement of blocks appears like threads
woven in and around each other. Directions on page 48.

Wyoming Valley Star by Sally Schneider, 1993, Puyallup, Washington, 67" x 85". Sally grew up in Pennsylvania's Wyoming Valley, and the making of this quilt became a journey through her memories. The colors used in each of the blocks remind her of particular events in her childhood. Quilted by Kari Lane. Directions on page 61.

Scrap Lumber by Sally Ambrose, 1993, Leavenworth, Washington, 58" x 58". Sally adapted an antique Tree pattern and arranged the trees so they rotated around the center. The background areas are quilted with leaves and acorns. Directions on page 66.

Spinning Stars by Sally Schneider, 1993, Puyallup, Washington, 47" x 59". The repeating stars here are the dull gold and the animal-print fabric. Using a light background fabric gives this quilt a more traditional look. Directions on page 58.

Midnight Stars by Linda Gabrielse, 1993, Grand Rapids, Michigan, 73" x 84". Dark navy background fabric and the rich, bright jewel tones of the stars give Linda's quilt a contemporary look. Directions on page 58.

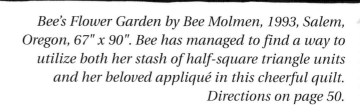

Bee's Flower Garden by Bee Molmen, 1993, Salem, Oregon, 67" x 90". Bee has managed to find a way to utilize both her stash of half-square triangle units and her beloved appliqué in this cheerful quilt. Directions on page 50.

Pinwheel Star by Sally Schneider, 1993, Puyallup, Washington, 58" x 78". This adaptation of a traditonal pattern uses Mary's Triangles for the star points, greatly simplifying construction. Quilted by Nancy Koorenny. Directions on page 92.

Lu's Flower Garden by Lu Storm, 1993, Bremerton, Washington, 39" x 49". Lu's use of beautiful floral prints for large triangles, and brown and green for the smaller triangles, looks like an old-fashioned garden with paths running through it. Lu used extra half-square triangle units to complete the border. Directions on page 78.

Sunshine and Shadows by Nancy J. Martin, 1989, Woodinville, Washington, 44" x 52". The consistent use of red fabrics for squares, and black and brown fabrics for the large triangles, make this a masculine-looking quilt. Collection of Nancy J. Martin. Directions on page 74.

MT Squared by Sally Schneider, 1993, Puyallup, Washington, 48" x 58". One of the many arrangements of the Mary's Triangles units that uses squares in the corner. This one is very similar to a traditional Log Cabin arrangement. Directions on page 74.

In Your Chain of Friendship, Consider ME a Link by Marnie Allard, 1993, Clearbrook, British Columbia, Canada, 66" x 74". A common background fabric and a "fabric menu" of green and blue make this a striking quilt. Marnie's initials are MEA; the ME can be found as printed-initial squares in two of the blocks. Directions on page 78.

MT Triangled by Sally Schneider, 1992, Puyallup, Washington, 42" x 50". Half-square triangle units in the block corners and a pinwheel arrangement provide a lively look. Directions on page 78.

Threads of Friendship by Margie Fisher, 1993, Thousand Oaks, California, 53" x 57". This Chain of Friendship arrangement of Mary's Triangles is a dynamic design. Margie's use of plaids softens the look and gives it a more comfortable feel. Directions on page 78.

Sarah's Fish by Barbara Eikmeier, 1993, Ft. Irwin, California, 65" x 85". Made for Barb's daughter, who chose many of the fish fabrics. Barb and Sarah got carried away on some of their fabric choices. You will find Red Fish, Blue Fish a la Dr. Seuss; several goldfish; parrot fish; angelfish; cowfish; and many more. Directions on page 82.

Rainbow Fish by Barbara Eikmeier, 1993, Ft. Irwin, California, 38" x 52". This quilt was made for Barb's son Eric, who commented after seeing the stipple quilting, "Mom, you scribbled all over my fish." Directions on page 82.

After Dark by Sally Schneider, 1993, Puyallup, Washington, 35" x 42". The screen saver program on my computer, After Dark™, is a fish design. After looking at those fish for a long time, I decided I had to make this quilt! It includes a "Painless Border." Directions on page 85.

Fall Trees by Sally Schneider, 1993, Puyallup, Washington, 37" x 45". A package of fat quarters in fall colors was the inspiration for this quilt. It even has the right red for my favorite sweet gum tree. Directions on page 87.

Summer Trees by Sally Schneider, 1993, Puyallup, Washington, 36" x 43". Mary's Triangles turned on end form this simple but lovely Tree pattern. It also has a "Painless Border." Quilted by Carol Anfinson. Directions on page 87.

Ocean Waves by Hawaii Quilt Guild, 1988, Honolulu, Hawaii, 76" x 94". One of the first Mary's Triangles workshops was taught to the Hawaii Quilt Guild, and this resulting quilt was their first raffle quilt. It was won by Barbara Eikmeier. Collection of Barbara Eikmeier. Directions on page 98.

Ocean Waves by Sally Schneider, 1993, Puyallup, Washington, 50" x 69". Quilted by Nancy Koorenny. Directions on page 98.

*Connley Lake by Tami Josties, 1993, Auburn, Washington,
69" x 85". One of a pair of quilts made for Tami's parents.
Directions on page 70.*

*Sweet Deal by Tami Josties, 1993, Auburn, Washington,
67" x 83". One of a pair of quilts made for Tami's parents.
Directions on page 70.*

Catherine Wheels

A simple pattern of squares and rectangles, this design was inspired by an antique quilt top owned by Cathy Hansen. Color photos: page 18.

FINISHED SIZE:

Crib 45½" x 53"
Lap 53" x 60½"
Twin 60½" x 90½"
Queen 83" x 98"

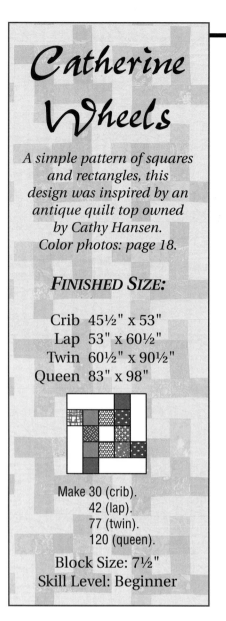

Make 30 (crib).
42 (lap).
77 (twin).
120 (queen).

Block Size: 7½"
Skill Level: Beginner

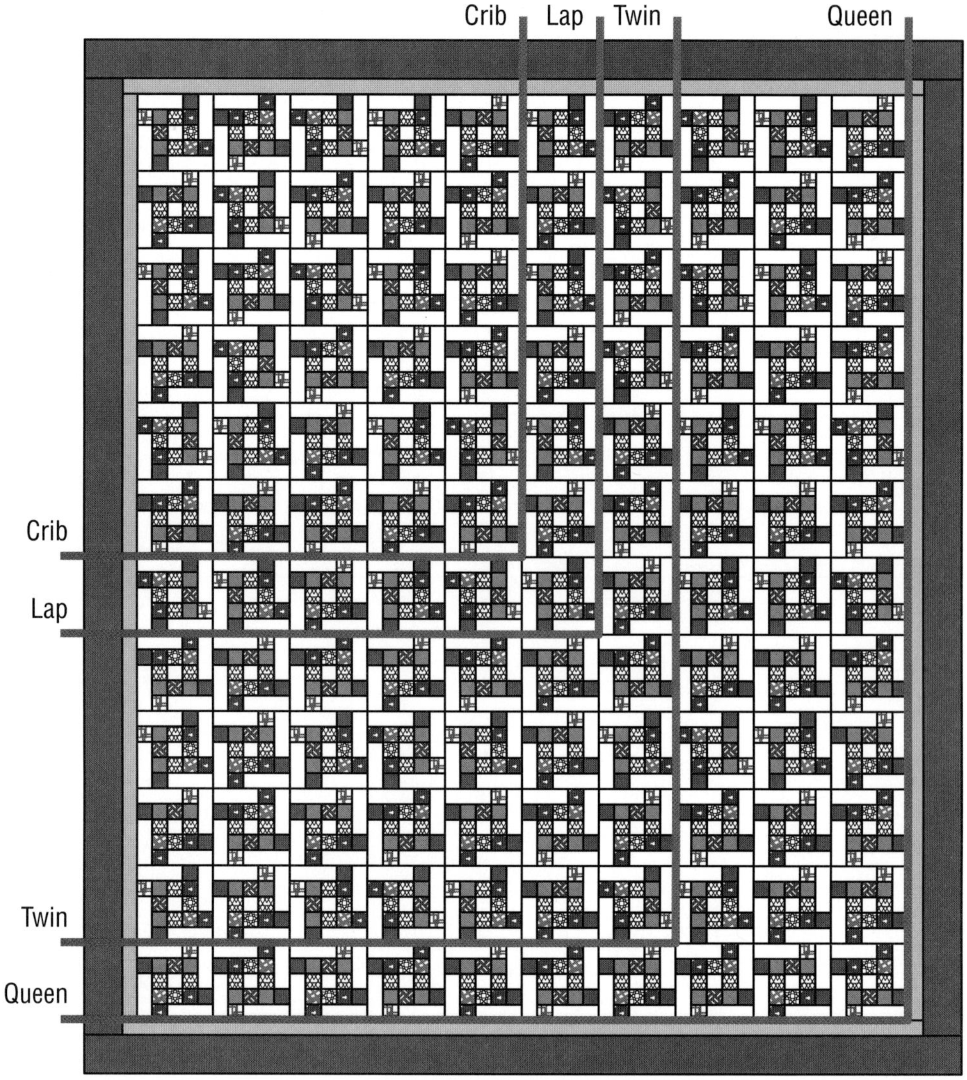

Fabric: *44" wide*				
	CRIB	LAP	TWIN	QUEEN
Background Fabric	1⅛ yds.	1½ yds.	2¾ yds.	4 yds.
2" x 22" Dark Strips	36	51	93	144
Inner Border	⅜ yd.	⅜ yd.	½ yd.	⅝ yd.
Outer Border	⅝ yd.	¾ yd.	1 yd.	1⅛ yd.
Backing	3 yds.	3½ yds.	5¼ yds.	7½ yds.
Batting	50" x 57"	57" x 65"	65" x 95"	87" x 102"
Binding	½ yd.	½ yd.	⅝ yd.	¾ yd.

Cutting

Fabric	FIRST CUT # Strips	FIRST CUT Strip Width	SECOND CUT # Pieces	SECOND CUT Dimensions
Crib Background	6	5"	120	2" x 5"
	2	2"	30	2" x 2"
Lap Background	8	5"	168	2" x 5"
	2	2"	42	2" x 2"
Twin Background	15	5"	308	2" x 5"
	4	2"	77	2" x 2"
Queen Background	23	5"	480	2" x 5"
	6	2"	120	2" x 2"

Block Assembly

1. Sew the 2" x 22" dark strips together into strip-pieced units of 3 strips each. Press seam allowances toward the center strip.

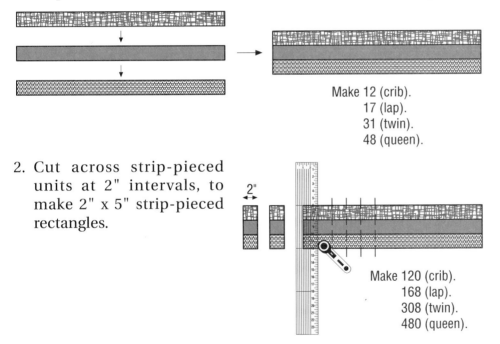

Make 12 (crib).
17 (lap).
31 (twin).
48 (queen).

2. Cut across strip-pieced units at 2" intervals, to make 2" x 5" strip-pieced rectangles.

2"

Make 120 (crib).
168 (lap).
308 (twin).
480 (queen).

3. Sew each strip-pieced rectangle to a background rectangle. Press seam allowances toward the background rectangle.

4. Join one 2" x 2" square of background fabric to one of the units made in step 3. Use a half seam as shown, leaving ¾" unattached.

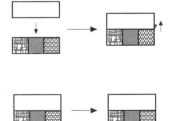

Note:

Add rectangles to successive sides of the unit in a clockwise direction only. Adding the units to the opposite ends will make the block appear to twist backwards.

5. Add another strip-pieced unit, joining the strip-pieced section to the end of the center square unit and matching seams as shown.

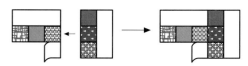

6. Sew another unit to the bottom of the block, matching seams.

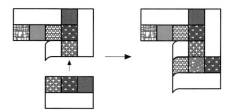

7. Sew another unit to the left side of the block.

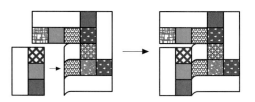

8. Matching seams, carefully pin and sew the remaining seam, starting at the 2" x 2" square and stitching to the block's outer edge. Repeat with the remaining units to make the number of blocks required for the quilt size you are making.

BLOCK SET	
Crib	5 x 6
Lap	6 x 7
Twin	7 x 11
Queen	10 x 12

Quilt Top Assembly

1. Arrange blocks into the required number of rows for the quilt size you are making.
2. Sew blocks together in rows, pressing seam allowances in opposite directions from row to row. Sew rows together.

BORDERS

Refer to "Borders" on pages 102–3 for cutting and measuring directions.

BORDER STRIPS		
	Inner Border 1½" wide	Outer Border 3½" wide
Crib	5	5
Lap	5	6
Twin	7	8
Queen	9	9

1. Cut the required number of inner and outer border strips and join as needed to make borders long enough for your quilt.
2. Measure the quilt top and cut borders.
3. Pin and sew borders to the quilt, adding the side borders first and then the top and bottom borders.

Quilt Finishing

Refer to the general finishing directions on pages 101–4.
1. Layer the quilt with batting and backing; baste.
2. Quilt as desired.
3. Bind the edges.

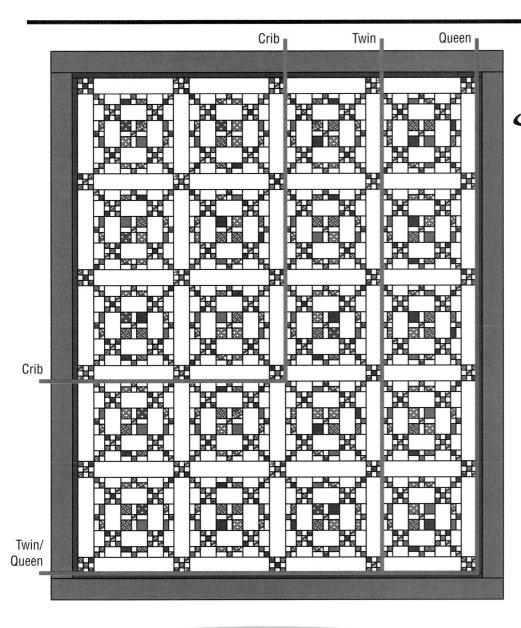

Crib Twin Queen

Crib

Twin/
Queen

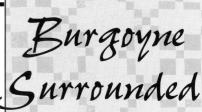

Burgoyne Surrounded

Always a favorite, Burgoyne Surrounded offers a variety of ways to use scraps. Select one fabric for the background to set off the scrappy pieces beautifully, or choose many subtly different background fabrics for a lovely dappled effect. Color photos: page 19.

FINISHED SIZE:

Crib 47" x 65"
Twin 65" x 101"
Queen 85" x 103"

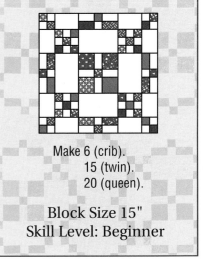

Make 6 (crib).
15 (twin).
20 (queen).

Block Size 15"
Skill Level: Beginner

Note:

You may choose 1½"-wide and 2½"-wide strips from your prepared pieces to replace the required dark and light fabrics. See the cutting chart for the number required. (See "Scrap Preparation," page 8.)

Fabric: *44" wide*

	CRIB	TWIN	QUEEN
Background Fabric	⅝ yds.	2 yds.	2⅜ yds.
9" x 22" Light Pieces	6	12	17
9" x 22" Dark Pieces	8	15	20
Sashing	1 yd.	2 yds.	2⅜ yds.
Inner Border	⅜ yd.	½ yd.	⅝ yd.
Outer Border	⅝ yd.	⅞ yd.	1¼ yds.
Backing	3 yds.	6 yds.	7½ yds.
Batting	51" x 69"	69" x 105"	89" x 107"
Binding	½ yd.	¾ yd.	¾ yd.

Cutting

Fabric	FIRST CUT # Strips	FIRST CUT Strip Width	SECOND CUT # Pieces	SECOND CUT Dimensions
Crib				
9" x 22" Light Pieces	20	1½"	—	1½" x 22"
	6	2½"	—	2½" x 22"
Background Fabric	3	3½"	48	3½" x 2½"
	4	3½"	24	3½" x 5½"
9" x 22" Dark Pieces	22	1½"	—	1½" x 22"
	8	2½"	—	2½" x 22"
Sashing	2	15½"	17	3½" x 15½"
Twin				
9" x 22" Light Pieces	46	1½"	—	1½ x 22"
	14	2½"	—	2½" x 22"
Background Fabric	8	3½"	120	3½" x 2½"
	9	3½"	60	3½" x 5½"
9" x 22" Dark Pieces	49	1½"	—	1½" x 22"
	20	2½"	—	2½" x 22"
Sashing	4	15½"	38	3½" x 15½"
Queen				
9" x 22" Light Pieces	60	1½"	—	1½" x 22"
	20	2½"	—	2½" x 22"
Background Fabric	10	3½"	160	3½" x 2½"
	12	3½"	80	3½" x 5½"
9" x 22" Dark Pieces	65	1½"	—	1½" x 22"
	26	2½"	—	2½" x 22"
Sashing	5	15½"	49	3½" x 15½"

Block Assembly

Strip-Pieced Units 1 and 2

1. Sew dark and light 1½"-wide strips together into strip-pieced unit variations shown below, using random dark and light strips.

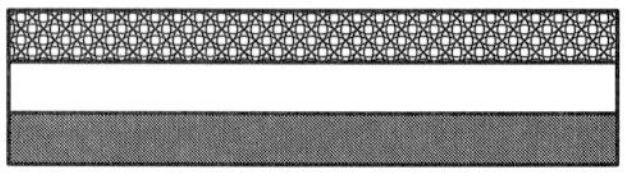

Strip-Pieced Unit 1
Make 6 (crib).
13 (twin).
17 (queen).

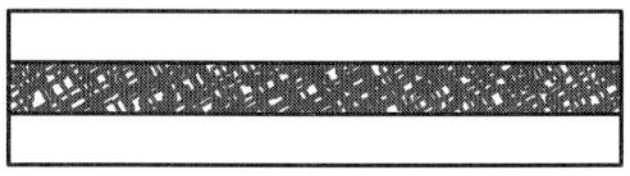

Strip-Pieced Unit 2
Make 3 (crib).
7 (twin).
9 (queen).

2. Crosscut at 1½" intervals to create rectangles.

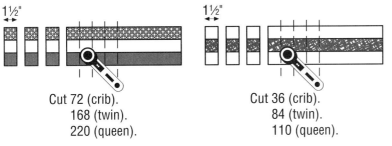

Cut 72 (crib).
168 (twin).
220 (queen).

Cut 36 (crib).
84 (twin).
110 (queen).

3. Sew the rectangles together to make Ninepatch blocks, mixing rectangles from different strip-pieced units. Make the number of blocks shown at right, reserving the required number of blocks for the sashing.

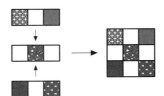

Ninepatch Block
Make 36; reserve 12 (crib).
84; reserve 24 (twin).
110; reserve 30 (queen).

Strip-Pieced Unit 3

1. Sew pairs of dark and light 1½"-wide strips together as shown below. Crosscut at 1½" intervals to create rectangles.

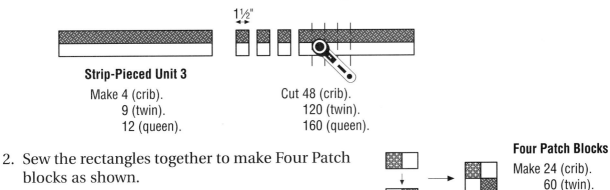

Strip-Pieced Unit 3
Make 4 (crib).
9 (twin).
12 (queen).

Cut 48 (crib).
120 (twin).
160 (queen).

2. Sew the rectangles together to make Four Patch blocks as shown.

Four Patch Blocks
Make 24 (crib).
60 (twin).
80 (queen).

Strip-Pieced Units 4 and 5

1. Sew two 2½"-wide strips to one 1½"-wide strip to make the 2 strip-pieced unit variations shown.

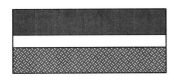

Strip-Pieced Unit 4
Make 4 (crib).
10 (twin).
13 (queen).

Strip-Pieced Unit 5
Make 3 (crib).
7 (twin).
10 (queen).

2. Crosscut strip-pieced Units 4 and 5 at 1½" intervals, cutting an equal number of rectangles from each set to get a variety of fabric combinations. Reserve the remaining strip-pieced units.

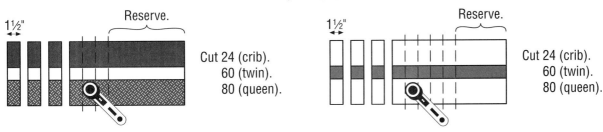

Cut 24 (crib).
60 (twin).
80 (queen).

Cut 24 (crib).
60 (twin).
80 (queen).

3. Sew rectangles together to make blocks as shown.

Make 24 (crib).
60 (twin).
80 (queen).

4. Crosscut the reserved strip-pieced Units 4 at 2½" intervals.

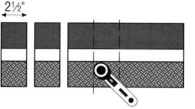

Cut 12 (crib).
30 (twin).
40 (queen).

5. Crosscut the reserved strip-pieced Units 5 at 1½" intervals.

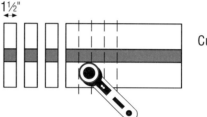

Cut 6 (crib).
15 (twin).
20 (queen).

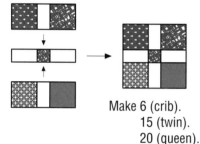

Make 6 (crib).
15 (twin).
20 (queen).

6. Sew rectangles together to make center blocks as shown at left.

Quilt Top Assembly

1. Assemble the blocks and background rectangles into rows as shown at right.
2. Sew the rows together to make blocks. Reserve extra Ninepatch blocks to use between sashing strips.

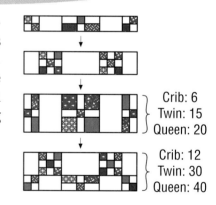

Crib: 6
Twin: 15
Queen: 20

Crib: 12
Twin: 30
Queen: 40

SASHING STRIPS

1. Sew the reserved Ninepatch blocks and the 3½"-wide sashing strips together as required for the quilt size you are making. Begin and end each row with a Ninepatch block.

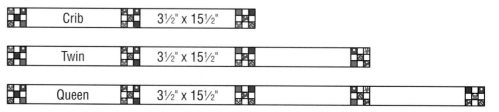

Crib   3½" x 15½"

Twin   3½" x 15½"

Queen   3½" x 15½"

2. Arrange the blocks into the required number of rows for the quilt size you are making. Sew blocks together in rows with sashing strips between each block. Sew a sashing strip to each end of each row.

BLOCK SET	
Crib	2 x 3
Twin	3 x 5
Queen	4 x 5

3. Sew rows together with sashing strips between. Sew a sashing strip to the top and bottom of the quilt.

BORDERS

Refer to "Borders" on pages 102–3 for cutting and measuring directions.
1. Cut the required number of inner and outer border strips and join as needed to make borders long enough for your quilt.
2. Measure the quilt top and cut borders.
3. Pin and sew borders to the quilt, adding the side borders first and then the top and bottom borders.

	BORDER STRIPS		
	Inner Border	Outer Border	
	1½" wide	3½" wide	4½" wide
Crib	5	5	
Twin	8	8	
Queen	9		9

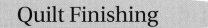

Quilt Finishing

Refer to the general finishing directions on pages 101–4.
1. Layer the quilt with batting and backing; baste.
2. Quilt as desired.
3. Bind the edges.

Friendship Stars

I used a large variety of background squares for this quilt. A 4½"-wide strip of fabric yields 9 squares, each measuring 4½" x 4½"; a fat quarter yields 12 squares. If you use just one background fabric, follow the yardage requirements listed below. Color photos: page 20.

FINISHED SIZE:

Wall 37" x 53"

Twin 69" x 85"

Queen 77" x 109"

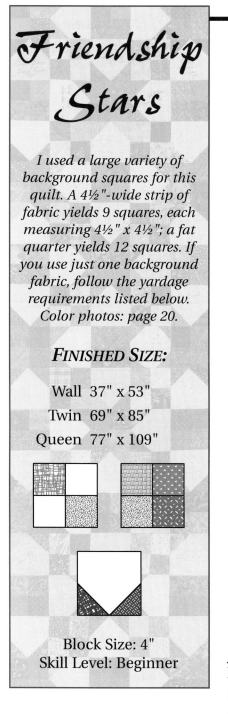

Block Size: 4"
Skill Level: Beginner

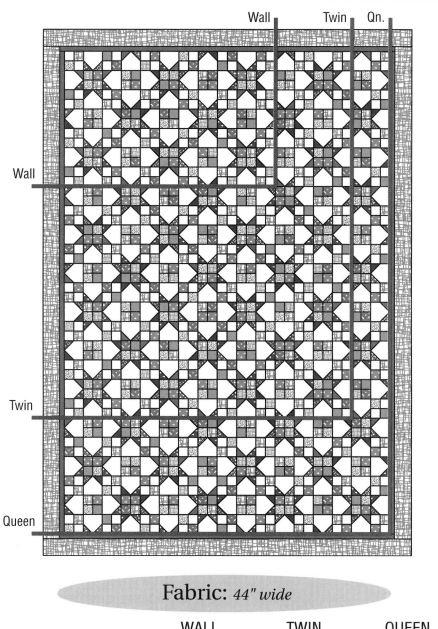

Fabric: *44" wide*

	WALL	TWIN	QUEEN
Background	¾ yd.	2¼ yds.	3 yds.
OR			
4½" Light Squares	38	142	212
2½" Dark Squares	76	284	424
2½" x 22" Light Strips	6	20	30
2½" x 22" Dark Strips	14	52	78
Inner Border	⅜ yd.	½ yd.	⅝ yd.
Outer Border	¾ yd.	1⅜ yds.	1¾ yds.
Backing	1⅝ yds.	5 yds.	7½ yds.
Batting	42" x 56"	74" x 90"	90" x 105"
Binding	½ yd.	⅝ yd.	¾ yd.

1. If you have used yardage, cut 4½" x 4½" squares from the background fabric.

2. Using the folded-corner technique on page 13, sew a 2½" square to a corner of a 4½" background square. Trim, leaving a ¼"-wide seam allowance. Sew another square to an adjacent corner; trim and press.

Note:

If you ask your friends to do these first two steps, you will have a good chance to increase the variety of fabrics used in your quilt! Have them sign, date, and write their hometown on their blocks.

Sally Schneider
1994
Puyallup, WA

3. Sew pairs of dark and light 2½" x 22" strips together as shown below. (Reserve the extra 2½" x 22" dark strips.) Press toward the dark strip. Crosscut at 2½" intervals to create rectangles.

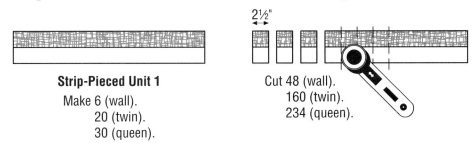

2½"

Strip-Pieced Unit 1

Make 6 (wall).
20 (twin).
30 (queen).

Cut 48 (wall).
160 (twin).
234 (queen).

4. Sew the rectangles together into Four Patch blocks as shown. Press.

Four Patch Block

Make 24 (wall).
80 (twin).
117 (queen).

5. Sew the remaining 2½" x 22" dark strips together in pairs. Press toward the darker strip. Crosscut at 2½" intervals to create rectangles. Press.

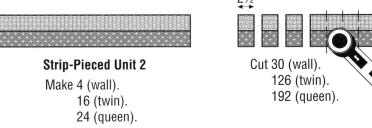

2½"

Strip-Pieced Unit 2

Make 4 (wall).
16 (twin).
24 (queen).

Cut 30 (wall).
126 (twin).
192 (queen).

6. Sew the rectangles together to make Four Patch blocks as shown. Press.

Four Patch Block

Make 15 (wall).
63 (twin).
96 (queen).

There are four alternating row arrangements for this quilt. Refer to the diagrams below for correct block placement.

1. Alternating the blocks and following the quilt plan on page 40, arrange into the required number of rows for the quilt size you are making.

Quilt Size	# Four Patch Blocks	# Folded Square Blocks	Block Arrangement
Wall	39	38	11 x 7
Twin	143	142	15 x 19
Queen	213	212	17 x 25

Note:

For both rows 1 and 2, rotate alternating folded corner blocks 180° within the row; rotate Four Patch blocks 90°.

Row 1: Begin and end with a Four Patch block.

Row 1

Row 2: Begin and end with a folded corner block.

Row 2

2. Sew the blocks together into rows. Press, then sew rows together, following diagram for placement. Press seam allowances in opposite directions from row to row.

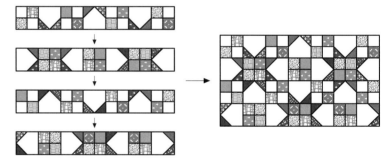

BORDERS

Refer to "Borders" on pages 102–3 for cutting and measuring directions.
1. Cut the required number of inner and outer border strips and join as needed to make borders long enough for your quilt.
2. Measure the quilt top and cut borders.
3. Pin and sew the borders to the quilt as shown on pages 102–3. Add the side borders first and then the top and bottom borders.

BORDER STRIPS

	Inner Border 1½" wide	Outer Border 3¾" wide
Wall	5	5
Twin	8	9
Queen	9	10

Quilt Finishing

Refer to the general finishing directions on pages 101–4.
1. Layer the quilt with batting and backing; baste.
2. Quilt as desired.
3. Bind the edges.

Queen Size

Wall Size

Off-Centered Log Cabin

By using both 1¼"- and 2½"-wide strips in a Log Cabin block, you can achieve the illusion of a curve without any complicated sewing. It is important to sew the wide strips to the center square first as shown in the diagrams below. If the wide and narrow strips are reversed, the curve is altered. Color photos: page 21.

FINISHED SIZE:

Wall 68" x 68"

Queen 91½" x 109"

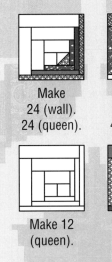

Make 24 (wall). 24 (queen).

Make 12 (wall). 40 (queen).

Make 12 (queen).

Make 4 (queen).

Block Size: 10¼" finished
Skill Level: Intermediate

	WALL	QUEEN
Dark Fabric (for half-square triangles)	⅜ yd.	½ yd.
Light Fabric (for half-square triangles)	⅜ yd.	½ yd.
2½" x 40" Dark Strips	15	56
2½" x 40" Light Strips	26	38
1¼" x 40" Dark Strips	31	36
1¼" x 40" Light Strips	17	65
2½" Dark Squares	–	4
2½" Light Squares	–	12
Border	⅞ yd.	1½ yds.
Backing	4⅛ yds.	8 yds.
Batting	73" x 73"	93" x 114"
Binding	⅝ yd.	⅞ yd.

Note:

You may choose 2½" cut (2" finished) half-square triangle units from your prepared pieces to replace the dark and light fabrics required for triangles. (See "Scrap Preparation," page 8.) See step 1 of "Block Assembly" below right for the number required.

Note:

Each step in the construction of Block 1 and Block 2 requires chain piecing. This technique saves time by sewing as many pieces together as possible without lifting the presser foot or cutting the thread between pieces. To chain piece the units for the following blocks, place each fabric strip right side up on the machine, then place each piece to be added on top, keeping right sides together. See illustration at right.

Block Assembly

1. Using dark and light fabrics, make the required number of 2" finished half-square triangle units for the quilt size you are making. If you use the grid method to make your half-square triangle units, the square you draw onto the grid should measure 2⅞". (See pages 14–15.) Press seam allowances toward the dark triangle.

 Make 36 (wall).
64 (queen).

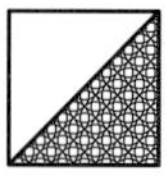

NUMBER OF GRIDS	
Wall	1½
Queen	3

2. Sew the first unit to the strip and without cutting the thread, set the next unit in place in front of the presser foot. Always keep the piece that you added to the block last nearest you as you place it on the strip. Lift the presser foot slightly, and slip the unit underneath, leaving a small space between the sewn unit and the new unit. Lower the presser foot and resume sewing.

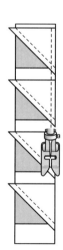

3. Continue joining units to strips, replacing strips as necessary until the desired number of units is sewn. Press, cut the units apart, and trim as directed on the next page.

Block 1

1. Choose the required half-square triangle units for the quilt size you are making. Sew each half-square triangle unit to a 2½"-wide light strip, chain piecing until all units are joined. Cut apart and trim as needed.

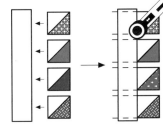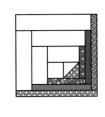

Block 1
Make 24 (wall).
24 (queen).

2. Place the newly sewn unit on top of another 2½"-wide light strip, positioning the half-square triangle unit at the top. Stitch, press, cut apart, and trim.

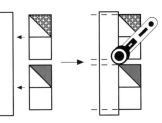

3. Turn the unit and add a 1¼"-wide dark strip to the unit as shown. Stitch, press, cut apart, and trim.

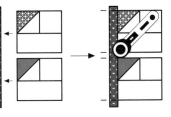

4. Turn again so that the last strip added is at the bottom and add another 1¼"-wide dark strip. Stitch, press, cut apart, and trim.

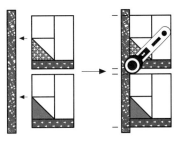

5. Repeat, turning units and adding strips, first wide light then narrow dark, until you have completed three rounds. End with the narrow dark strips. Press, cut apart, and trim after adding each new strip. See Block 1 diagram above.

Block 2

1. Choose the required half-square triangle units for the quilt size you are making. Join each half-square triangle unit to a 2½"-wide dark strip, chain piecing until all units are joined. Press, cut apart, and trim the strip even with each half-square triangle unit as shown.

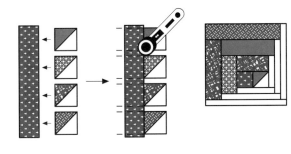

Block 2
Make 12 (wall).
40 (queen).

2. Place the newly sewn unit on top of another 2½"-wide strip of dark fabric, positioning the half-square triangle unit to be sewn first. Stitch, press, cut apart, and trim as shown.

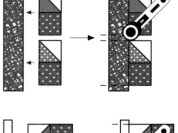

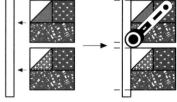

3. Turn the unit and sew a 1¼"-wide light strip to the unit as shown. Press, cut apart, and trim.

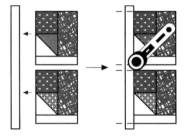

4. Turn again so that the last strip you added is at the bottom. Add another narrow 1¼"-wide light strip. Press, cut apart, and trim.

5. Continue turning units and adding strips, first wide dark then narrow light, until you have completed 3 rounds. Press, cut apart, and trim after adding each new strip. End with the narrow dark strips. See Block 2 diagram on page 45.

Include the following 2 blocks in the Queen-size version only.

Blocks 3 and 4

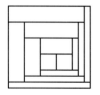

Block 3
Make 12 (queen).

Block 4
Make 4 (queen).

1. For Block 3: Use twelve 2½" light squares in place of the half-square triangle units. Follow the steps for Block 1 on page 45, using all light-colored strips. Remember to keep all the 2½"-wide strips on one-half of the block and all the 1¼"-wide strips on the other half. Press after adding each new strip.

2. For Block 4: Use four 2½" dark squares in place of the half-square triangle units. Follow the steps for Block 1 on page 45, using all dark-colored strips. Remember to keep all the 2½"-wide strips on one-half of the block and all 1¼"-wide strips on the other half. Press after adding each new strip.

Quilt Top Assembly

1. Arrange the blocks as shown in the diagram for the quilt size you are making.
2. Sew blocks together into rows, pressing seams in opposite directions from row to row. Sew rows together.

BORDERS

Refer to "Borders" on pages 102–3 for cutting and measuring directions.

1. Cut the required number of border strips and join strips as needed to make borders long enough for your quilt.
2. Measure the quilt top and cut borders.
3. Pin and sew borders to the quilt, adding the side borders first and then the top and bottom borders.

Note:

The queen-size quilt has two different border widths; sew a 5"-wide border to each side, and a 3½"-wide border to the top and bottom.

BORDER STRIPS		
	3½" wide	5" wide
Wall	7	—
Queen	5	5

Quilt Finishing

Refer to the general finishing directions on pages 101–4.

1. Layer the quilt with batting and backing; baste.
2. Quilt as desired.
3. Bind the edges.

Interweave

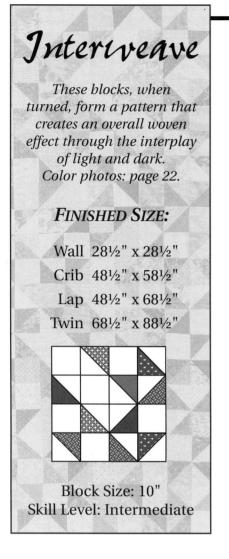

These blocks, when turned, form a pattern that creates an overall woven effect through the interplay of light and dark. Color photos: page 22.

FINISHED SIZE:

Wall 28½" x 28½"

Crib 48½" x 58½"

Lap 48½" x 68½"

Twin 68½" x 88½"

Block Size: 10"
Skill Level: Intermediate

Note:

You may choose 3½" cut (3" finished) half-square triangle units from your prepared pieces to replace the light and dark fabrics required for triangles. (See "Scrap Preparation," page 8.)

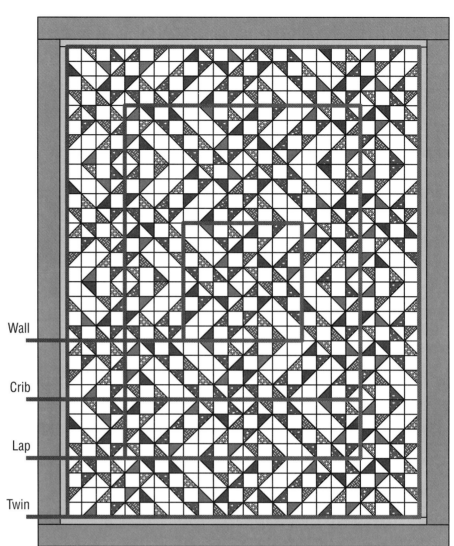

Wall

Crib

Lap

Twin

Fabric: *44" wide*

	WALL	CRIB	LAP	TWIN
Dark Fabric* (for half-square triangles)	⅜ yd.	1 yd.	1⅜ yds.	2¼ yds.
Light Fabric* (for half-square triangles)	⅜ yd.	1 yd.	1⅜ yds.	2¼ yds.
3" x 22" Light Strips	4	18	21	42
Inner Border	¼ yd.	⅜ yd.	⅜ yd.	½ yd.
Outer Border	½ yd.	¾ yd.	⅞ yd.	1⅛ yds.
Backing	⅞ yd.	3 yds.	3 yds.	5½ yds.
Batting	32" x 32"	62" x 62"	52" x 72"	72" x 92"
Binding	¼ yd.	½ yd.	½ yd.	1 yd.

*Or use scraps.

Cutting

1. Using dark and light fabrics, make the required number of 2½" finished half-square triangle units for the quilt size you are making. If you use the grid method for constructing half-square triangle units, draw 3⅜" grid squares. Press seam allowances toward the dark triangle. (See page 11.)
2. From the 3"-wide strips of light fabric, cut the required number of 3" squares for the quilt size you are making.

WALL	CRIB	LAP	TWIN
24	120	144	288

Make 40 (wall).
200 (crib).
240 (lap).
480 (twin).

NUMBER OF GRIDS	
Wall	2
Crib	8½
Lap	10
Twin	20

Block and Quilt Top Assembly

1. Arrange squares and half-square triangle units into blocks as shown.

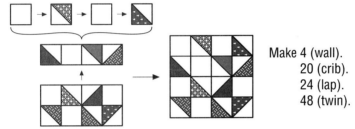

Make 4 (wall).
20 (crib).
24 (lap).
48 (twin).

Note:

Each block has a large, light diagonal area. In the diagram, find each light area to help you orient each block properly.

BLOCK SET	
Wall	2 x 2
Crib	4 x 5
Lap	4 x 6
Twin	6 x 8

2. Arrange the blocks into the required number of rows for the quilt size you are making. Refer to the quilt plan for block arrangement.
3. Sew blocks together into rows, pressing seam allowances in opposite directions from row to row. Sew rows together.

BORDERS

Refer to "Borders" on pages 102-3 for cutting and measuring directions.
1. Cut the required number of inner and outer border strips and join as needed to make borders long enough for your quilt.
2. Measure the quilt top and cut borders.
3. Pin and sew borders to the quilt, adding the side borders first and then the top and bottom borders.

	BORDER STRIPS	
	Inner Border 1½" wide	Outer Border 3½" wide
Wall	4	4
Crib	5	6
Lap	6	7
Twin	8	9

Quilt Finishing

Refer to the general finishing directions on pages 101–4.
1. Layer the quilt with batting and backing; baste.
2. Quilt as desired.
3. Bind the edges.

Bee's Flower Garden

When my friend Bee Molmen showed me her quilt using this pattern I knew immediately that it was perfect for all of us scrap "maniacs" who also like simple appliqué. To simplify construction, directions are given for large triangles to replace the smaller triangles around the edges of the quilt pictured on page 25. The quilt photographed is a size between the twin and queen quilt described in the directions.
Color photo: page 25.

FINISHED SIZE:

Crib	36½" x 49½"
Lap	49¼" x 62"
Twin	62" x 87½"
Queen	87½" x 100¼"

Make	Make
6 (crib).	2 (crib).
12 (lap).	6 (lap).
24 (twin).	15 (twin).
42 (queen).	30 (queen).

Block Size: 9"
Skill Level: Intermediate
Templates: page 57

Crib   Lap   Twin

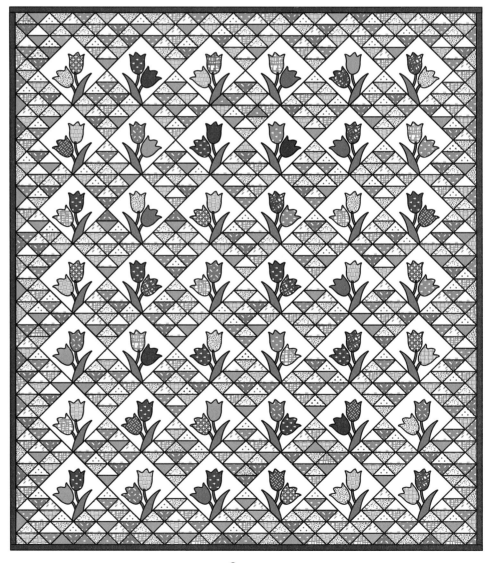

Queen

Fabric: 44" wide

	CRIB	LAP	TWIN	QUEEN
Tulip Fabrics (total scraps)	⅛ yd.	¼ yd.	½ yd.	⅞ yd.
Leaf and Stem Fabrics (total scraps)	⅛ yd.	¼ yd.	¼ yd.	½ yd.
Appliqué Background	¾ yd.	1 yd.	1⅞ yds.	3⅜ yds.
Piping	⅜ yd.	⅜ yd.	¾ yd.	1¼ yds.
Light Fabric* (for half-square triangles)	1⅛ yds.	1¼ yds.	2 yds.	2½ yds.
Dark Fabric* (for half-square triangles and edge triangles)	1⅛ yds.	1¾ yds.	2½ yds.	3¼ yds.
Border	¼ yd.	⅜ yd.	½ yd.	½ yd.
Backing	1½ yds.	3 yds.	5 yds.	7½ yds.
Batting	38" x 50"	50" x 63"	63" x 88"	88" x 100"
Binding	⅜ yd.	½ yd.	⅝ yd.	¾ yd.

Or use scraps. Yardage requirements are given to make half-square triangle units if you do not use prepared units.

Note:

Choose 3½" cut (3" finished) half-square triangle units from your prepared pieces to replace the dark and light fabrics required for triangles. (See "Scrap Preparation," page 8.)

Appliqué Block Assembly

Hand appliqué the Tulip blocks, using your favorite method, or follow directions below for machine appliquéing the tulips, leaves, and stems.

1. Make a plastic template for each pattern piece on page 57. Trace around templates onto the dull side of the freezer paper. On the lines you drew, cut the number of freezer-paper pattern pieces required for the quilt size you are making.
2. From appliqué background fabric, cut the number of 10"-wide strips required for the quilt size you are making. Crosscut into the required number of 10" squares.
3. Following directions for invisible machine appliqué (or using your favorite appliqué method), lay out and appliqué pieces as shown.

4. Trim the completed blocks to 9½" x 9½".

APPLIQUÉ BLOCKS

	# 10" Strips	# Squares
Crib	2	6
Lap	3	12
Twin	6	24
Queen	11	42

Note:

Appliqué all Tulip blocks identically or reverse the pattern in alternating vertical rows as shown in the color photo on page 25.

PIPING		
	# 9½" Strips	# ¾" x 9½" Strips
Crib	1	24
Lap	1	48
Twin	2	96
Queen	3	168

5. For piping, cut the number of 9½"-wide strips of fabric required for the quilt size you are making. Crosscut into the required number of ¾" x 9½" strips.

6. Fold each strip in half lengthwise, wrong sides together, and press.

7. Sew 1 strip to each side of each block in numerical order, matching the raw edges of the piping strips with the raw edges of the block.

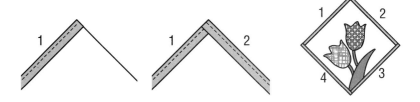

INVISIBLE MACHINE APPLIQUÉ

Prepare the Pieces

1. Wash and iron all fabric. Use 100% cottons.

2. Trace all templates required onto the dull (uncoated) side of freezer paper. Cut out freezer paper along the lines you traced; do not add seam allowances.

Note:

If more than one piece is required, you may fold the freezer paper into layers and staple it, then cut up to four layers at a time. Since this technique produces two sets of mirror images, it will only work if the pieces are symmetrical or face opposite directions.

Note:

If several appliqué pieces are cut from the same pattern, press one freezer-paper pattern to the fabric, fold or stack the fabric, and cut out up to four layers at a time. Iron the remaining freezer-paper patterns onto the cut fabric pieces.

3. Iron the shiny side of the freezer-paper pattern onto the wrong side of the fabric.

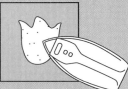

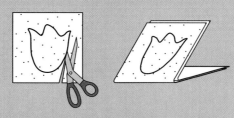

4. Cut out fabric with ³⁄₁₆"-wide seam allowance (halfway between ⅛" and ¼").

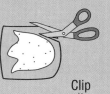

5. Clip inside points. Clip deep concave curves if necessary, but clip them only halfway to the edge of the freezer paper.

6. Rub a water-soluble glue stick around the edges of the fabric and paper.

7. Roll the seam allowance over the edge of the freezer paper and stick it in place, making sure there are no pleats or puckers. Ease them out if necessary.

8. On sharp points, such as the base of a heart or the point of a leaf, fold the fabric over the point, then fold over the remaining seam allowances as shown.

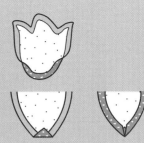

9. Mark the background for placement if desired. Place a piece of fabric stabilizer on the back of the background square. This adds stability to the fabric and helps prevent puckering. Pin the pieces to the background, or use a water-soluble glue stick.

Attach the Pieces

1. Set your machine for the blind hem stitch. Use a size 60/8 or 70/10 needle.

2. Attach an open-toe appliqué foot.

Open-toe appliqué foot

3. Fill the bobbin with 100% cotton lightweight thread. (DMC Machine Embroidery thread is good.)

4. Thread the top of the machine with invisible nylon thread.

5. Set the stitch width to about 1½; set the stitch length to very short—about 20 stitches per inch.

6. Check the tension on a piece of scrap fabric. You should not be able to see any bobbin thread on the top piece. It is usually necessary to loosen the top tension. (Dial down to a smaller number.)

7. On the bottom layer of fabric, starting on one long side if possible, stitch around each piece with the stitching line running just outside of the appliquéd piece. The occasional zigzag stitches should just catch the fabric of the appliquéd piece.

8. When you get to the points, zigzag a few stitches in place. Do the same thing at inside points, reinforcing these spots.

9. After all appliqué pieces are stitched in place, cut out background fabric from behind them, leaving a ¼"-wide seam allowance.

10. Wet the piece, soaking a few minutes if necessary, and gently remove the freezer paper from the back of the appliqués. Use tweezers on the hard-to-reach places.

11. Allow to dry. Using a low-heat setting, gently press the piece from the back side. Pressing from the front may melt the nylon thread.

Pieced Block Assembly

Make 104 (crib).
176 (lap).
311 (twin).
500 (queen).

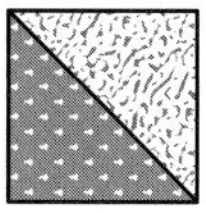

NUMBER OF GRIDS	
Crib	4½
Lap	7½
Twin	13
Queen	21

1. Using the light and dark fabrics and your favorite method, make 3½" half-square triangle units, or construct them using the grid method as directed on pages 14–15. Draw 3⅞" grid squares.

2. Sew half-square triangle units together into Ninepatch blocks as shown below. Make the number of blocks required for the quilt size you are making. Set aside the remaining half-square triangle units for the edge and corner units below.

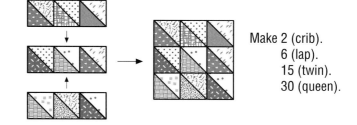

Make 2 (crib).
6 (lap).
15 (twin).
30 (queen).

Edge and Corner Units

CUTTING CHART		
	# 6"-wide Strips	# 6" Squares
Crib	2	9
Lap	2	12
Twin	3	16
Queen	3	21

1. From dark scrap fabric, cut the number of 6"-wide strips required for the quilt size you are making. Crosscut into 6" x 6" squares.

2. Cut each 6" x 6" square twice diagonally to make the required number of edge triangles for the quilt size you are making.

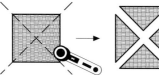

Cut 34 triangles (crib).
46 triangles (lap).
64 triangles (twin).
82 triangles (queen).

3. From the remaining fabric, cut 2 squares, 4" x 4". Cut in half once diagonally for the corner setting triangles.

4. Arrange half-square triangle units and dark edge triangles to make left, right, top, and bottom edge units as shown below. Pay attention to the light and dark triangle placement in the diagrams. Each unit requires 9 half-square triangle units and 3 dark edge triangles.

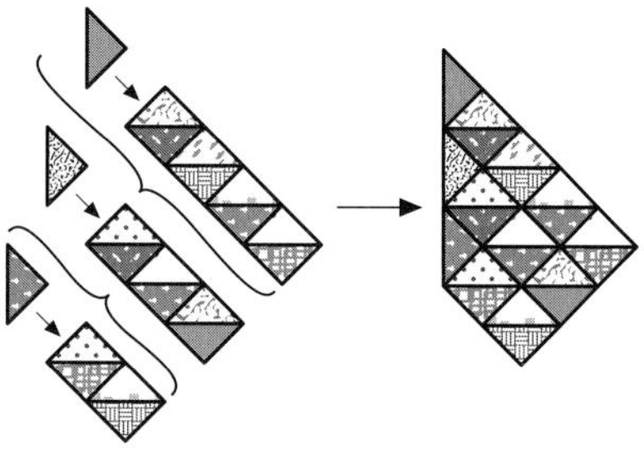

Left Edge Unit
Make 2 (crib).
3 (lap).
5 (twin).
6 (queen).

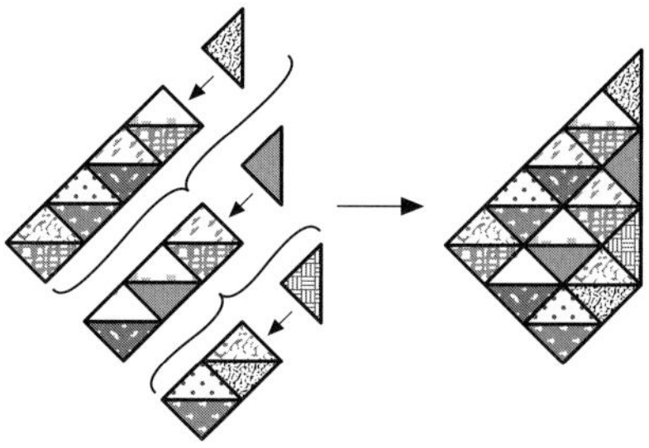

Right Edge Unit
Make 2 (crib).
3 (lap).
5 (twin).
6 (queen).

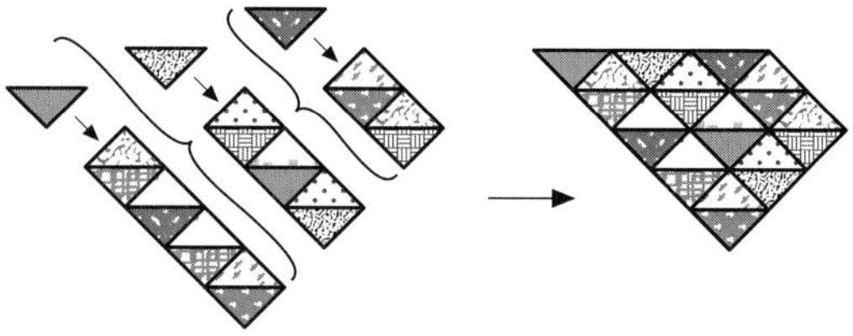

Top Edge Unit
Make 1 (crib).
2 (lap).
3 (twin).
5 (queen).

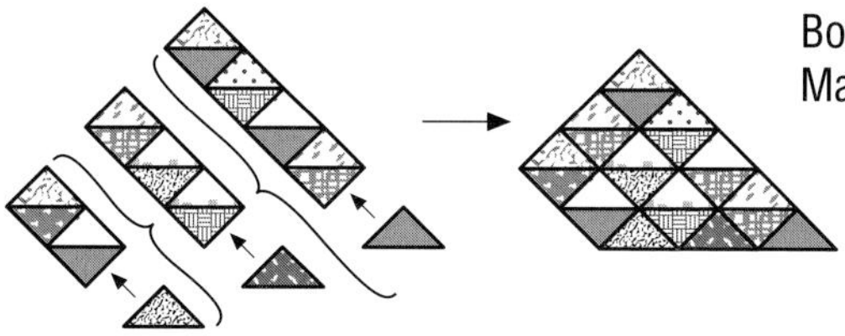

Bottom Edge Unit
Make 1 (crib).
2 (lap).
3 (twin).
5 (queen).

5. For the lower left and upper right corner units, arrange 9 half-square triangle units, 6 dark edge triangles, and 1 corner setting triangle for each unit as shown below. Pay careful attention to the light and dark triangle placement.

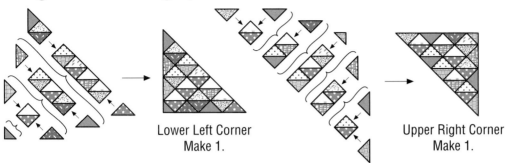

Lower Left Corner
Make 1.

Upper Right Corner
Make 1.

6. For lower right and upper left corner units, arrange 7 half-square triangle units, 2 dark edge triangles, and a corner setting triangle. Pay careful attention to the light and dark triangle placement.

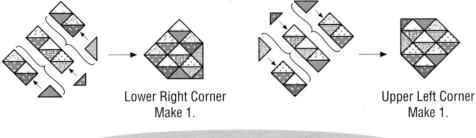

Lower Right Corner
Make 1.

Upper Left Corner
Make 1.

Quilt Top Assembly

1. Arrange appliqué blocks, half-square triangle blocks, and pieced side and corner units as shown in the quilt plan.

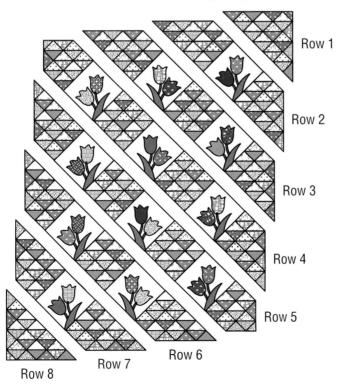

Row 1

Row 2

Row 3

Row 4

Row 5

Row 6

Row 7

Row 8

2. Beginning at the upper right corner, sew blocks and pieced units together in diagonal rows. (See "Diagonal Settings" on pages 100–101.) Press seam allowances in opposite directions from row to row.
3. Sew the rows together.

BORDERS

Refer to "Borders" on pages 102–3 for cutting and measuring directions.
1. Cut the required number of 1½"-wide border strips and join as needed to make borders long enough for your quilt.
2. Measure the quilt top and cut borders.
3. Pin and sew borders to the quilt, adding the side borders first and then the top and bottom borders.

BORDER STRIPS

Crib	4
Lap	6
Twin	8
Queen	9

Quilt Finishing

Refer to the general finishing directions on pages 101–4.
1. Layer the quilt with a batting and backing; baste.
2. Quilt as desired.
3. Bind the edges.

Bee's Flower Garden Templates

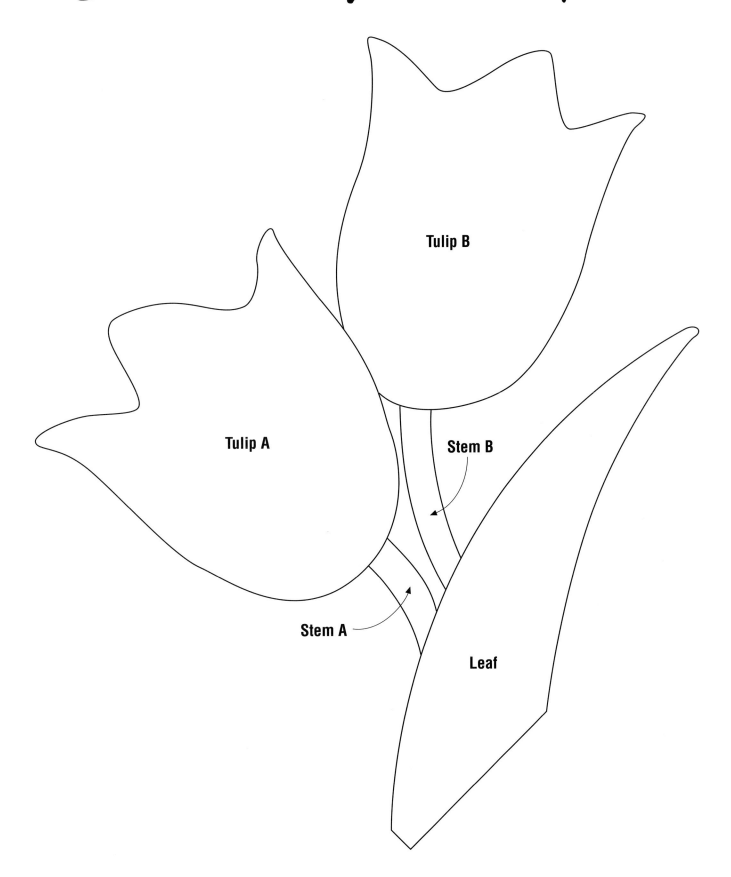

Tulip B

Tulip A

Stem B

Stem A

Leaf

Spinning Stars

Spinning Stars is a traditional pattern that I have adapted for scraps by using a "fabric recipe" technique. In Spinning Stars blocks, the two opposite corners' parallelograms (A) are one color while the other two corners' parallelograms (B) are a different color. Although the fabrics vary from block to block, these colors remain the same throughout the quilt. The remaining parallelograms (C) are always the same color within one block but differ in color from block to block. The triangles are always the same value.
Color photos: page 24.

FINISHED SIZE:

Lap 46½" x 58½"

Twin 70½" x 94½"

Full 82½" x 94½"

Queen 94½" x 106½"

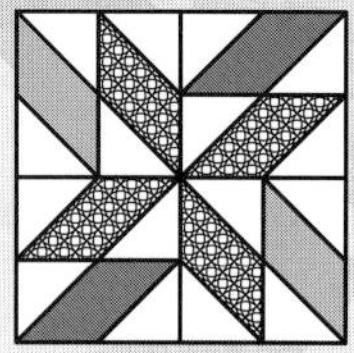

Make 12 (lap).
35 (twin).
42 (full).
56 (queen).

Block Size: 12"
Skill Level: Beginner

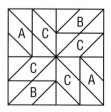

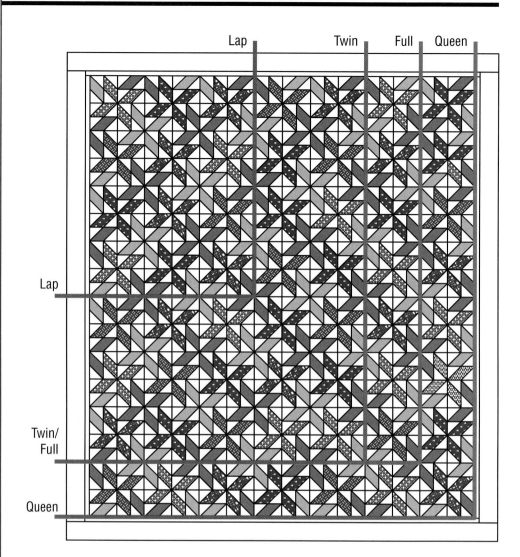

Fabric: *44" wide*				
	LAP	TWIN	FULL	QUEEN
Background	1¾ yds.	4⅞ yds.	5¾ yds.	7¾ yds.
Star Color A	¾ yd.	1¼ yds.	1½ yds.	2 yds.
Star Color B	¾ yd.	1¼ yds.	1½ yds.	2 yds.
Star Color C (¼ yd. Pieces)	12	18	21	28
Inner Border	⅜ yd.	½ yd.	½ yd.	⅝ yd.
Outer Border	¾ yd.	1¼ yds.	1⅜ yds.	1⅜ yds.
Backing	3 yds.	6 yds.	7½ yds.	9 yds.
Batting	50" x 62"	74" x 98"	86" x 98"	98" x 110"
Binding	½ yd.	⅝ yd.	¾ yd.	¾ yd.

Cutting

Fabric	FIRST CUT # Strips	FIRST CUT Strip Width	SECOND CUT # Pieces	SECOND CUT Dimensions
Lap				
Background	16	3½"	192	3½" x 3½"
Star Color A	2	6½"	24	3½" x 6½"
Star Color B	2	6½"	24	3½" x 6½"
Star Color C	1 ea. color	6½"	4 ea. color	3½" x 6½"
Twin				
Background	47	3½"	560	3½" x 3½"
Star Color A	6	6½"	70	3½" x 6½"
Star Color B	6	6½"	70	3½" x 6½"
Star Color C	1 ea. color	6½"	8 ea. color	3½" x 6½"
Full				
Background	56	3½"	672	3½" x 3½"
Star Color A	7	6½"	84	3½" x 6½"
Star Color B	7	6½"	84	3½" x 6½"
Star Color C	1 ea. color	6½"	8 ea. color	3½" x 6½
Queen				
Background	75	3½"	896	3½" x 3½"
Star Color A	10	6½"	112	3½" x 6½"
Star Color B	10	6½"	112	3½" x 6½"
Star Color C	1 ea. color	6½"	8 ea. color	3½" x 6½"

Block Assembly

1. Following the directions for folded corners on page 13, sew a background square to both ends of each 3½" x 6½" rectangle to create a parallelogram unit. Make sure that both seams are sewn in the same direction.

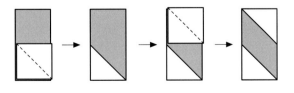

2. Separate units into groups—one group of Color A, another of Color B, and groups of 8 of each Color C. (The lap quilt version will have groups of 4 of each Color C.)

Note:

For a rectangle with a folded corner plus a half-square triangle unit, stitch another seam ½" away from the first seam as directed for folded corners on page 13. Cut between the sewn lines. Use this sewn half-square triangle unit for a border or for another quilt.

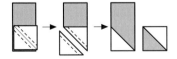

3. For each block, sew a Color C unit to a Color A unit. Make 2. Sew each of the remaining Color C units to a Color B unit. Press seam allowances toward the Color C unit.

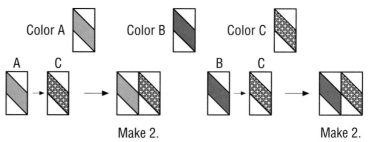

Make 2.   Make 2.

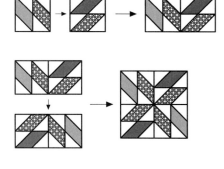

4. Rotate each Color B/C unit and join to an A/C unit as shown at left, matching seams where necessary. Press seam allowances toward the A/C unit.
5. Sew block halves together as shown at left, matching seams carefully.

6. Arrange the blocks into the required number of rows for the quilt size you are making. Rotate the blocks if necessary to place Color A and Color B in position to form secondary stars.

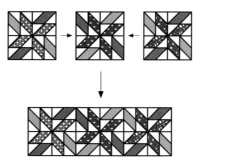

BLOCK SET	
Lap	3 x 4
Twin	5 x 7
Full	6 x 7
Queen	7 x 8

Note:

When sewing blocks together, seam allowances twist when matching points. When this occurs, clip the seam allowance on the diagonal almost to the stitching line and press the two seam-allowance sections in opposite directions.

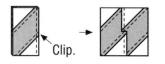

Clip.

7. Sew blocks into rows, pressing seam allowances in opposite directions from row to row. Sew rows together.

BORDERS

Refer to "Borders" on pages 102–3 for cutting and measuring directions.
1. Cut the required number of inner and outer border strips and join as needed to make borders long enough for your quilt
2. Measure the quilt top and cut borders.
3. Pin and sew borders to the quilt, adding the side borders first and then the top and bottom borders.

BORDER STRIPS

	Inner Border 1½" wide	Outer Border 4½" wide
Lap	5	5
Twin	8	9
Full	9	9
Queen	10	10

Quilt Finishing

Refer to the general finishing directions on pages 101–4.
1. Layer the quilt with batting and backing; baste.
2. Quilt as desired.
3. Bind the edges.

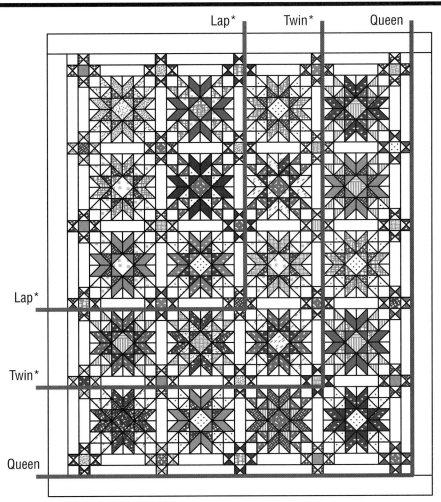

* The lap and twin quilt versions have sashing strips on the right and bottom edges as does the queen size.

Wyoming Valley Star

Coordinated fabrics make up each Wyoming Valley Star block, but each block differs from the others within the quilt. The only fabric repeated throughout the quilt is the background. Color photo: page 23.

FINISHED SIZE:

Lap 50" x 68"
Twin 68" x 85"
Queen 85" x 103"

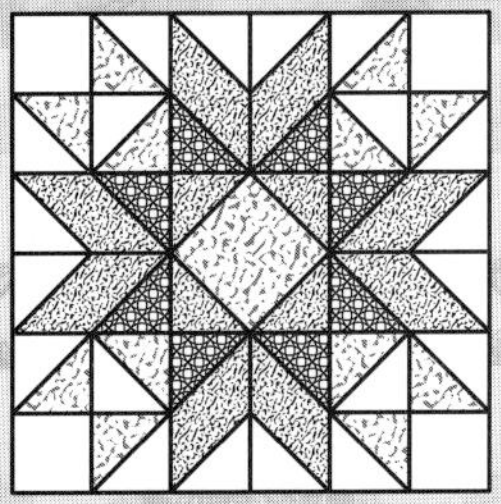

Make 6 (lap).
12 (twin).
20 (queen).

Block Size: 15"
Skill Level: Intermediate

Fabric: *44" wide*

	LAP	TWIN	QUEEN
Background (includes sashing)	2½ yds.	4 yds.	6 yds.
9" x 22" Dark Pieces	6	12	20
18" x 22" Medium Pieces	6	12	20
9" x 22" Light-Medium Pieces	6	12	20
3" x 3" Dark Squares (for Ohio Star centers)	12	20	30
3¾" x 3¾" Dark Squares (for Ohio Star points)	2 squares of 12 fabrics	2 squares of 20 fabrics	2 squares of 30 fabrics
Borders	⅞ yd.	1¼ yds.	1⅜ yds.
Backing	3⅛ yds.	5 yds.	7½ yds.
Batting	54" x 72"	72" x 90"	90" x 108"
Binding	⅝ yd.	⅝ yd.	¾ yd.

Block Cutting

	FIRST CUT		SECOND CUT	
	#Strips	Strip Width	#Pieces	Dimensions
Lap				
Dark (9" x 22" pieces)	7	3"	48	3" x 3"
Medium (18" x 22" pieces)	16	3"	48	3" x 5½"
			24	3" x 3"
Light Medium (9" x 22" pieces)	*	*	6	5½" x 5½"
Background	6	3"	76**	3" x 3"
Twin				
Dark (9" x 22"pieces)	14	3"	96	3" x 3"
Medium (18" x 22" pieces)	31	3"	96	3" x 5½"
			48	3" x 3"
Light Medium (9" x 22" pieces)	*	*	12	5½" x 5½"
Background	11	3"	148**	3" x 3"
Queen				
Dark (9" x 22"pieces)	23	3"	160	3" x 3"
Medium (18" x 22" pieces)	52	3"	160	3" x 5½"
			80	3" x 3"
Light Medium (9" x 22"pieces)	*	*	20	5½" x 5½"
Background	18	3"	244**	3" x 3"

*For each block, cut the 5½" x 5½" light-medium square from the same fabric as the light-medium fabric in the half-square triangle units.
**Reserve 4 squares for borders.*

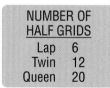

NUMBER OF
HALF GRIDS
Lap   6
Twin 12
Queen 20

Make 12 per block.
Total: 72 (lap).
144 (twin).
240 (queen).

Block Assembly

1. Using background fabric and each light-medium fabric, construct half grids for 2½" finished half-square triangle units as directed on pages 14–15. For the twin and queen sizes only: Draw half grids on background fabric with the long sides parallel to the selvage edges, to fit 5 half grids across the fabric. Draw grid squares 3⅜" x 3⅜". Each half grid yields 12 half-square triangle units, enough for 1 block. Press seam allowances toward the darker fabric.

2. Place a 3" square of background fabric at one end of a 3" x 5½" medium rectangle, as shown at right. Following the directions for folded corners on page 13, stitch in one direction from corner to corner for 4 units and stitch in the opposite direction from corner to corner for the 4 remaining units. Press.

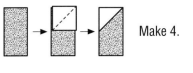

Make 4.

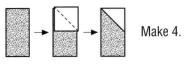

Make 4.

3. Repeat step 2, using the 3" dark squares and sewing them to the other end of the rectangles as shown.

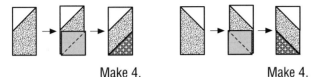

Make 4.   Make 4.

4. Sew these units together as shown.

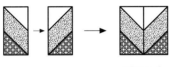

Make 4.

5. For the center unit, use the folded-corner technique, placing a 3" square of medium fabric at two opposite corners of a light-medium 5½" square. Stitch, trim, and press. Repeat with the remaining two corners.

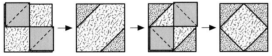

6. For each corner unit, join 3 half-square triangle units and 1 background 3" square as shown below.

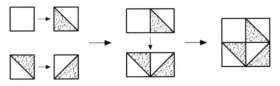

7. Arrange units as shown in the diagram below. Sew units together into rows, then sew rows together. Make the number of blocks required for the quilt size you are making.

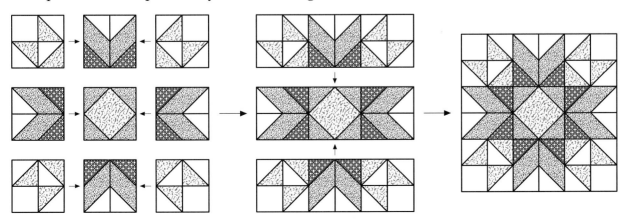

Sashing and Ohio Stars Setting Squares

Cutting

Fabric	FIRST CUT # Strips	FIRST CUT Strip Width	SECOND CUT # Pieces	SECOND CUT Dimensions
Lap Background	2	10½"	17	3" x 10½"
	1	15½"	10	3" x 15½"
	3	3¾"	24	3¾" x 3¾"
Twin Background	3	10½"	31	3" x 10½"
	1	15½"	14	3" x 15½"
	4	3¾"	40	3¾" x 3¾"
Queen Background	4	10½"	49	3" x 10½"
	2	15½"	18	3" x 15½"
	6	3¾"	60	3¾" x 3¾"

Assembly

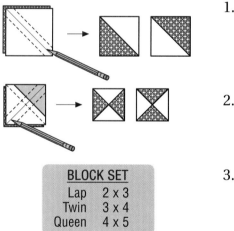

BLOCK SET
Lap	2 x 3
Twin	3 x 4
Queen	4 x 5

1. Referring to "Quarter-Square Triangle Units" on page 15, layer the 3¾" dark squares right sides together with the 3¾" background squares. Draw a diagonal line through the center of the background square; sew ¼" away on both sides of the line. Cut on the line; press seams to the darker side.

2. Place 2 matching half-square triangle units right sides together. Draw a diagonal line on the back of 1 square, crossing the seam. Stitch ¼" away on both sides of the drawn line; cut on the line. Press units.

3. Referring to the quilt plan on page 61, lay out the blocks, 10½" and 15½" sashing strips, quarter-square triangle units, and 3" x 3" dark squares. Make sure to use 4 matching quarter-square triangle units for each Ohio Star.

4. Sew quarter-square triangle units to each end of the 10½" sashing strips as shown.

5. Sew a vertical sashing strip to the left side of each block, adding a sashing strip at the end of each row.

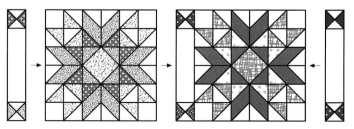

6. Join blocks in horizontal rows as shown. Sew a 3" x 15½" vertical sashing strip to each end.

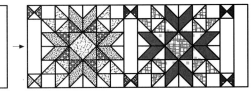

7. Sew 3" dark fabric squares to horizontal sashing strips. Sew a quarter-square triangle unit to each end. Make sure to match quarter-square triangle units to make Ohio Stars.

8. For the top and bottom sashing strip, sew 1 quarter-square triangle unit to each 3" x 15½" sashing strip. Sew a quarter-square triangle unit to 1 end and a 3" background square to each end as shown.

9. Sew rows together.

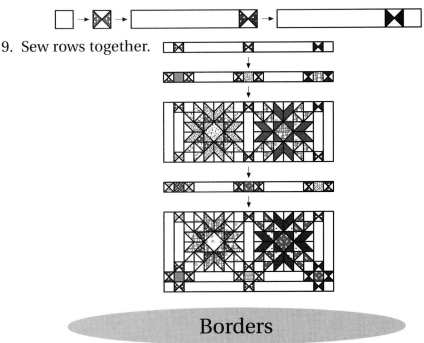

Borders

Refer to "Borders" on pages 102–3 for cutting and measuring directions.
1. Cut 4½"-wide strips as needed for border and join to make borders long enough for your quilt.
2. Measure the quilt top and cut borders.
3. Pin and sew borders to the quilt, adding the side borders first and then the top and bottom borders.

BORDER STRIPS

Lap	5
Twin	7
Queen	9

Quilt Finishing

Refer to the general finishing directions on pages 101–4.
1. Layer the quilt with batting and backing; baste.
2. Quilt as desired.
3. Bind the edges.

Scrap Lumber

Create this stunning wall hanging using 2" (finished) half-square triangle units from your box of cutaways. Color photo: page 23.

FINISHED SIZE:

68" x 68"

Block Size: 20"
Skill Level: Intermediate

Note:

You may choose 2" finished half-square triangle units from your prepared pieces to replace the 9" x 22" pieces of light and dark fabrics. (See "Scrap Preparation," page 8.)

Fabric: *44" wide*

2½" x 2½" Half-Square Triangle Units	316
9" x 22" Light Pieces* (for half-square triangle units)	14*
9" x 22" Dark Pieces* (for half-square triangle units)	14*
2½" x 2½" Medium Squares	28
Background	2¾ yds.
Inner Border	⅝ yd.
Outer Border (optional)	1¼ yds.
Backing	4⅛ yds.
Batting	72" x 72"
Binding	⅝ yd.

Use these light and dark pieces to construct half grids for half-square triangle units if you do not use prepared units. See Step 1 of Block Assembly on page 67.

Cutting

Background Fabric	FIRST CUT		SECOND CUT	
	# Strips	Strip Width	# Pieces	Dimensions
Units 4 and 7	2	4½"	8	4½" x 6½"
Units 1 and 10	4	2½"	8	2½" x 8½"
			28	2½" x 2½"
	1	18"	2	18" x 18"
	4	8½"	4	8½" x 40½"

Block Assembly

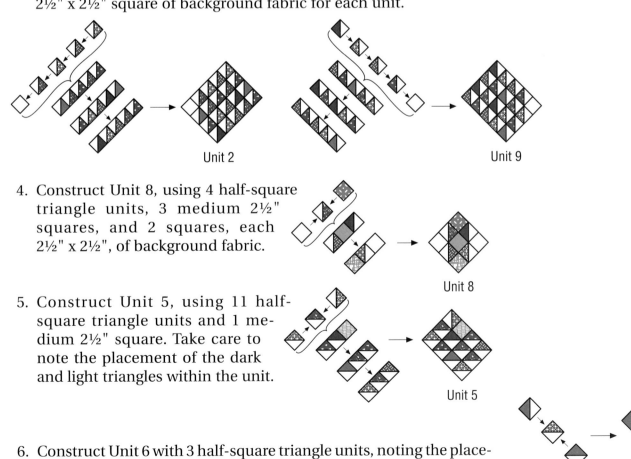

1. If you do not use already-prepared half-square triangle units, construct 27 half grids from the dark and light fabrics to make 316 half-square triangle units, following the instructions on pages 14–15. On your grid, draw a 2⅞" square to yield 2" finished half-square triangle units.

2. Construct Unit 3, using 12 half-square triangle units, 3 medium 2½" squares, and a 2½" x 2½" square of background fabric.

3. Construct Units 2 and 9, using 19 half-square triangle units and a 2½" x 2½" square of background fabric for each unit.

Unit 3

Unit 2

Unit 9

4. Construct Unit 8, using 4 half-square triangle units, 3 medium 2½" squares, and 2 squares, each 2½" x 2½", of background fabric.

Unit 8

5. Construct Unit 5, using 11 half-square triangle units and 1 medium 2½" square. Take care to note the placement of the dark and light triangles within the unit.

Unit 5

6. Construct Unit 6 with 3 half-square triangle units, noting the placement of the dark and light triangles within the unit.

Unit 6

7. Arrange the completed units for each block and join into units 1/2/3, 4/5, 6/7/8, and 9/10 as shown. Join the units to complete the block.

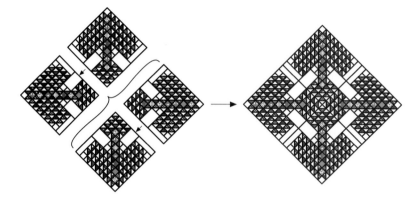

Quilt Top Assembly

1. Join the 4 blocks, with each tree's base at the center.

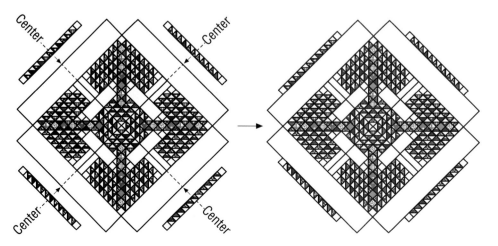

2. Sew an 8½" x 40½" strip to each side of the quilt.

3. Sew 11 half-square triangle units into a strip. Add a 2½" light square to each end.

Make 4.

4. Sew a half-square triangle strip to each 8½" x 40½" background strip, carefully matching centers.

5. Cut the two 18" squares of background fabric in half diagonally.
6. Sew the long side of each triangle to each row of half-square triangle units, matching centers.

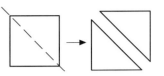

Make 4.

7. Square and trim the quilt's edges.

BORDERS

Refer to "Borders" on pages 102–3 for cutting and measuring directions.
1. Cut the required number of inner and outer border strips and join strips as needed to make borders long enough for your quilt.
2. Measure the quilt top and cut borders.
3. Pin and sew borders to the quilt, adding the side borders first and then the top and bottom borders.

BORDER STRIPS	
Inner Border 2" wide	Outer Border 4 1/2" wide
8	8

Quilt Finishing

Refer to the general finishing directions on pages 101–4.
1. Layer the quilt with batting and backing; baste.
2. Quilt as desired.
3. Bind the edges.

1,000 Pyramids

This pattern is a popular choice for scrap quilts, making it possible to use many leftover fabrics from other projects. Cut equilateral triangles individually from scraps, or quickly piece this quilt using the method for making 60° diamonds described below. Color photo: page 31.

FINISHED SIZE:

Crib 33" x 56"

Twin 54" x 96"

Queen 84" x 96"

Make 209 (crib).
540 (twin).
690 (queen).

Equilateral Triangle Size:
3¾"

Skill Level: Intermediate

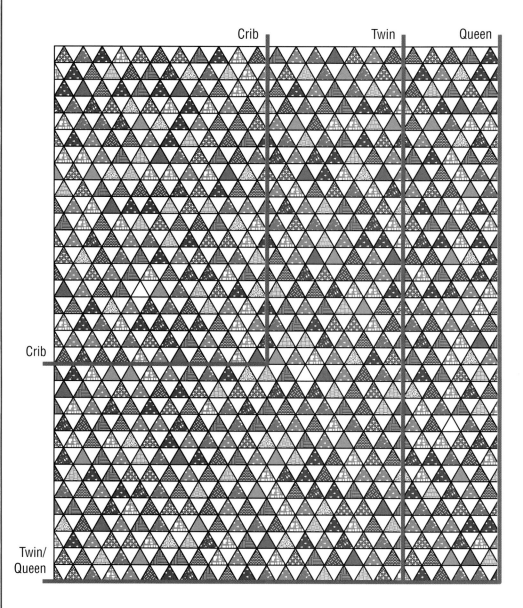

Crib

Twin

Queen

Crib

Twin/
Queen

Fabric: *44" wide*

	CRIB	TWIN	QUEEN
9" x 22" Dark Pieces	14	34	44
9" x 22" Light Pieces	14	34	44
Backing	1¾ yds.	6 yds.	8 yds.
Batting	45" x 60"	90" x 108"	90" x 108"
Binding	⅜ yd.	½ yd.	⅝ yd.

Equilateral Triangle Grids

Use this method to quickly piece equilateral triangles into 60° diamonds. Arrange the pieced diamonds to your liking, sew them together into rows, and then sew the rows together to finish the quilt. This is a good place to use some of your fat quarters!

1. Draw parallel lines spaced 4" apart on the back of the lighter of two fabrics.

2. Align the 60° line of a 6" x 24" ruler along one of the drawn lines. Draw a new line and continue drawing lines 4" apart.

3. Align the ruler in the other direction and connect points to complete the triangles.

4. Place the marked fabric right sides together with a darker piece of fabric.

5. Stitch ¼" away on both sides of each line that runs from the top left to the bottom right.

6. Cut the grid apart on each of the lines that you have drawn.

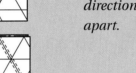

7. Gently pull the tips of the triangles apart to remove the stitches. Press seam allowances toward the darker diamonds.

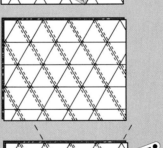

Pull apart here to remove stitch and open triangle pair.

8. Reserve the partial diamonds remaining at the ends of the rows for use at the ends of the quilt rows.

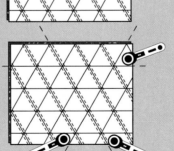

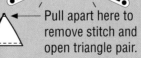

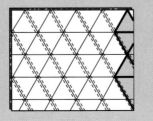

Note:

Always use dark and light values when layering two fabrics.

Note:

For smaller diamonds, use a smaller grid; for larger diamonds, use a larger grid. Draw the lines in all three directions the same distance apart.

Note:

A pair of fat eighths (9" x 22") yields approximately 16 diamonds. A pair of fat quarters (18" x 22") yields approximately 32 diamonds.

BLOCK SET	
Crib	11 x 19
Twin	18 x 30
Queen	23 x 30

1. Make the number of diamonds required for the quilt size you are making (see box on page 70), following directions for Equilateral Triangle Grids on page 71.
2. Arrange the diamonds in a pleasing way into the required number of rows for the quilt size you are making. Alternate dark and light triangles; place reserved partial diamonds at the ends of the rows.

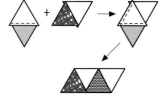

3. Sew the diamonds together into rows. To sew the diamonds accurately, line up 2 diamonds, placing the triangles exactly on top of each other and matching raw edges. Stitch, using a ¼"-wide seam allowance. Press toward the dark triangle.
4. Repeat, sewing diamonds in groups of 4, then in groups of 8 and so forth for the number of diamonds needed to complete each horizontal row. Sew a reserved partial triangle to each end of the row as needed.

Sew into groups of 4, then join groups.

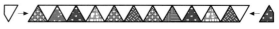

Add partial triangles as needed.

5. Sew rows together, matching the points of the diamonds. (Match points as for eight-point centers. See Strip-Pieced Unit Construction on pages 12–13)
6. Trim the uneven edges. Be sure to leave a ¼"-wide seam allowance beyond the finished points of the diamonds.

Quilt Finishing

Refer to the general finishing directions on pages 101–4.
1. Layer the quilt with batting and backing; baste.
2. Quilt as desired.
3. Bind the edges.

Mary's Triangles

Those of you who are traditional quilters may recognize the block I call Mary's Triangles as a Shaded Four Patch made of a square, two small triangles, and one large triangle.

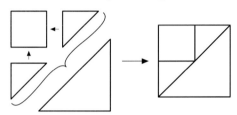

This versatile block can be sewn in three different colorations, then set in many ways to create patterns well suited to scrap quilts.

While the block is not new, the assembly method given in this book departs from tradition, creating two blocks at a time instead of one.

A variation of this block replaces the square with a half-square triangle unit, creating more opportunity for value interplay. The following quilt patterns require the Mary's Triangles blocks and provide suggestions for alternate settings. There are even ways to create fish and trees using these blocks!

Mary's Triangles with Squares

These simple units can be used to make many different patterns. See page 77 for a variety of different block-setting options. Color photos: page 26.

FINISHED SIZE:

Crib 40½" x 56½"

Lap 48½" x 72½"

Twin 64½" x 88½"

Queen 80½" x 96½"

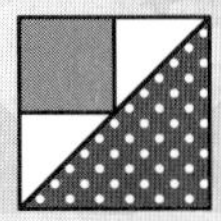

Make 96 (crib).
160 (lap).
280 (twin).
396 (queen).

Block Size: 4"
Skill Level: Beginner

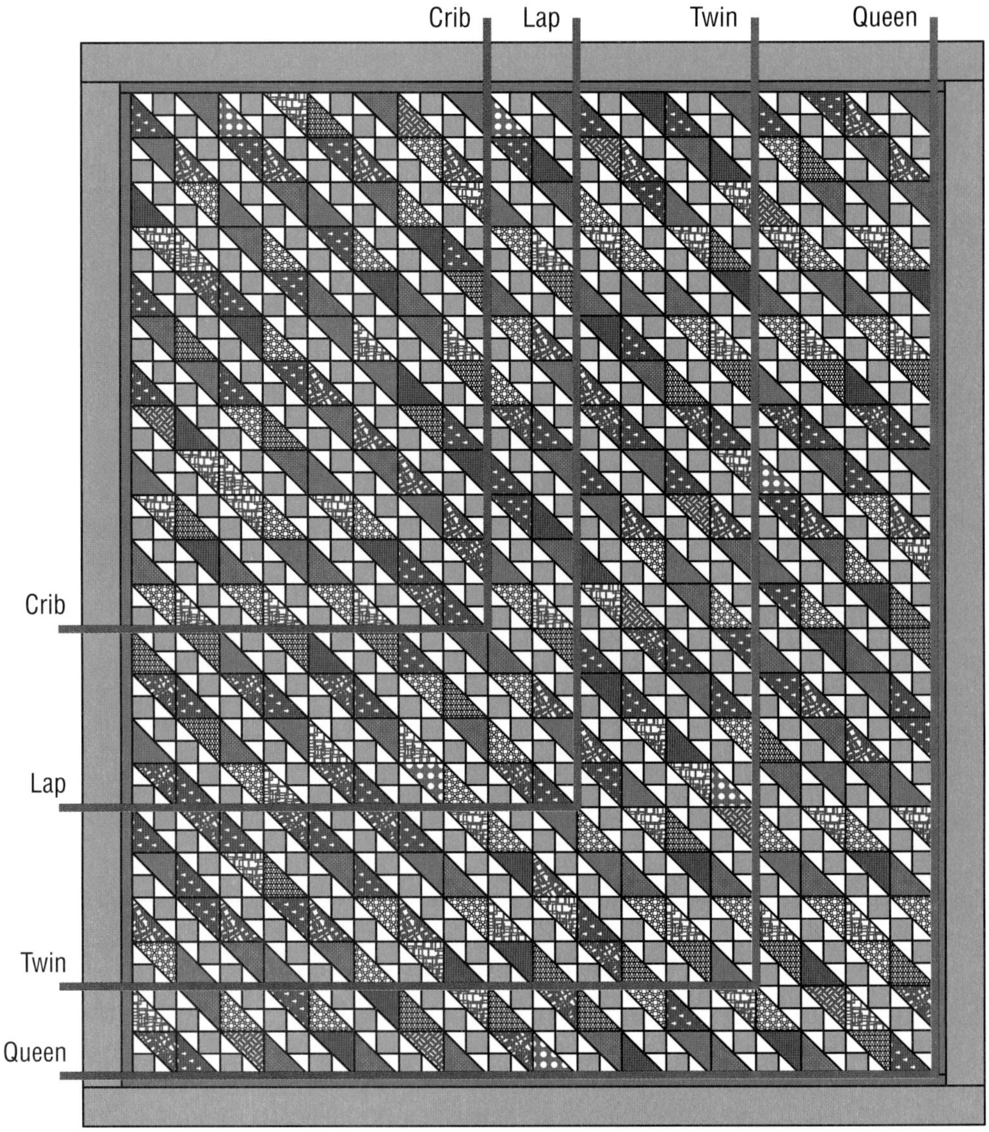

Fabric: *44" wide*				
	CRIB	LAP	TWIN	QUEEN
9" x 22" Dark Pieces*	10	16	30	39
9" x 22" Light Pieces*	6	8	14	19
Inner Border	⅜ yd.	½ yd.	½ yd.	⅝ yd.
Outer Border	¾ yd.	⅞ yd.	1¼ yds.	1⅜ yds.
Backing	2½ yds.	3 yds.	5¼ yds.	7¼ yds.
Batting	44" x 60"	52" x 76"	68" x 92"	84" x 100"
Binding	½ yd.	½ yd.	⅝ yd.	¾ yd.

Or use scraps.

Cutting

	FIRST CUT		SECOND CUT	
	# Strips	Strip Width	# Pieces	Dimensions
Crib				
9" x 22" Dark Fabrics	12	2½"	96	2½" x 2½"
	12	4½"	48	4½" x 5½"
9" x 22" Light Fabrics	16	2½"	96	2½" x 3½"
Lap				
9" x 22" Dark Fabrics	20	2½"	160	2½" x 2½"
	20	4½"	80	4½" x 5½"
9" x 22" Light Fabrics	27	2½"	160	2½" x 3½"
Twin				
9" x 22" Dark Fabrics	35	2½"	280	2½" x 2½"
	35	4½"	140	4½" x 5½"
9" x 22" Light Fabrics	47	2½"	280	2½" x 3½"
Queen				
9" x 22" Dark Fabrics	50	2½"	396	2½" x 2½"
	50	4½"	198	4½" x 5½"
9" x 22" Light Fabrics	66	2½"	396	2½" x 3½"

Block Assembly

1. Following the illustrations below, sew each 2½" x 3½" light rectangle to a 2½" dark square.

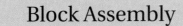

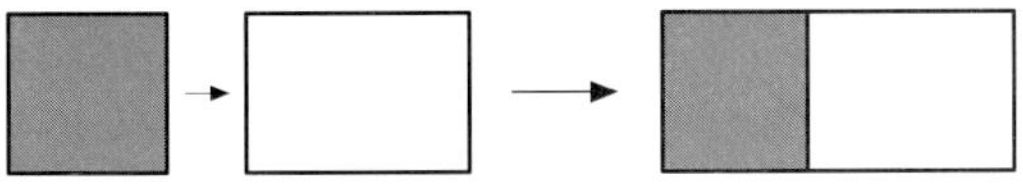

2. Sew pairs of these units together as shown. Clip the seam allowance to the seam line in the center so that you can press the seam away from the squares in opposite directions as shown.

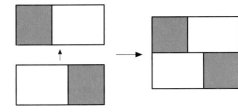
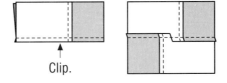

Clip.

3. Cut a 4½" square of template material, then cut the square in half diagonally.

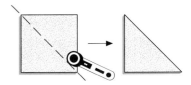

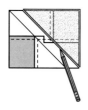

4. Place the template on the wrong side of the pieced unit with the corner of the template matching the outer corner of each square. Draw a diagonal line along the long edge of the template. Rotate the template to the opposite corner of the unit and draw a second line as shown at left.

5. Place a 4½" x 5½" dark rectangle right sides together with each pieced rectangle in the desired arrangement. Stitch on each of the drawn lines. Cut between them, creating 2 blocks as shown below.

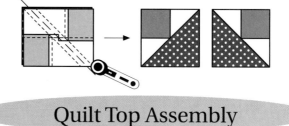

Quilt Top Assembly

BLOCK SET	
Crib	8 x 12
Lap	10 x 16
Twin	14 x 20
Queen	18 x 22

1. Arrange the blocks into the required number of rows for the quilt size you are making. Refer to the Block Setting Options on page 73 or design your own setting.

2. Sew blocks together in rows, pressing seams in opposite directions from row to row. Sew rows together.

BORDERS

Refer to "Borders" on pages 102-3 for cutting and measuring directions

BORDER STRIPS		
	Inner Border 1½" wide	Outer Border 3½" wide
Crib	5	5
Lap	6	7
Twin	7	8
Queen	8	9

1. Cut the required number of inner and outer border strips and join as needed to make borders long enough for your quilt.

2. Measure the quilt top and cut borders.

3. Pin and sew borders to the quilt, adding the side borders first and then the top and bottom borders.

Quilt Finishing

Refer to the general finishing directions on pages 101–4.

1. Layer the quilt with batting and backing; baste.

2. Quilt as desired.

3. Bind the edges.

Block Setting Options

Mary's Triangles with Triangles

Half-square triangle units may be substituted for the squares in this variation of Mary's Triangles. Remember to alternate values when these units are used. Color photos: pages 26, 27.

FINISHED SIZE:

Crib	40" x 56"
Lap	48" x 72"
Twin	64" x 88"
Queen	80" x 96"

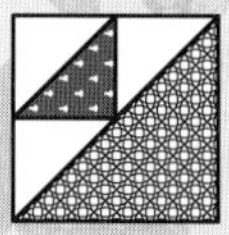

Make 96 (crib).
160 (lap).
280 (twin).
396 (queen).

Block Size: 4"
Skill Level: Beginner

Note:

You may choose 2½" cut half-square triangle units and 2½" and 5½" strips from your prepared pieces to replace the dark and light fabrics required. (See "Scrap Preparation," page 8.) See the cutting chart for the number required.

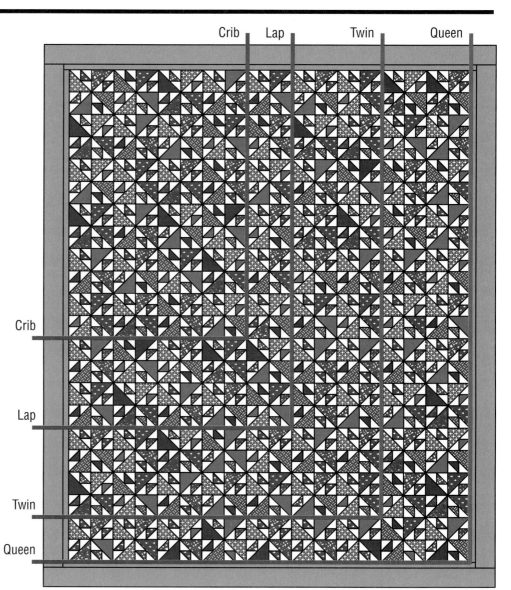

Fabric: *44" wide*				
	CRIB	LAP	TWIN	QUEEN
9" x 22" pieces (dark)	10	17	30	42
Background (light)	1¼ yds.	2¼ yds.	3¼ yds.	4¼ yds.
Inner Border	⅜ yd.	½ yd.	½ yd.	⅝ yd.
Outer Border	¾ yd.	⅞ yd.	1¼ yds.	1⅜ yds.
Backing	2½ yds.	3 yds.	5¼ yds.	7¼ yds.
Batting	44" x 60"	52" x 76"	68" x 92"	84" x 100"
Binding	½ yd.	½ yd.	⅝ yd.	¾ yd.

Cutting

1. Using dark and light fabrics, make the required number of 2½" x 2½" half-square triangle units for the quilt size you are making. If you use the grid method of making half-square triangle units, draw 2⅞" grid squares. See pages 14–15 for complete directions.

2. Following the chart below, cut the required pieces from the remaining fabric. Cut all dark strips across the length of each 9" x 22" piece of fabric.

Make 96 (crib).
160 (lap).
280 (twin).
396 (queen).

2½" x 2½" cut

NUMBER OF GRIDS	
Crib	4
Lap	7
Twin	12
Queen	16½

Fabric	FIRST CUT # Strips	Strip Width	SECOND CUT # Pieces	Dimensions
Crib				
Background Fabric (Light)	8	2½"	96	2½" x 3½"
Dark Fabric*	12	4½"	48	4½" x 5½"
Lap				
Background Fabric (Light)	14	2½"	160	2½" x 3½"
Dark Fabric*	20	4½"	80	4½" x 5½"
Twin				
Background Fabric (Light)	24	2½"	280	2½" x 3½"
Dark Fabric*	35	4½"	140	4½" x 5½"
Queen				
Background Fabric (Light)	33	2½"	396	2½" x 3½"
Dark Fabric*	50	4½"	198	4½" x 5½"

All dark strips are 22" long.

Block Assembly

1. Sew the light 2½" x 3½" rectangles to dark half-square triangle units as shown below.

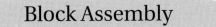

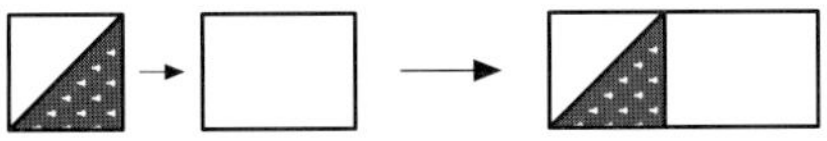

2. Sew pairs of these units together as shown. Clip the seam allowance to the seam line in the center so that you can press seams away from the half-square triangle units.

Clip.

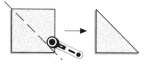

3. Cut a 4½" square of template material, then cut the square in half diagonally.

4. Place the template on the wrong side of each pieced unit. Match the template corner to the outer corner of one of the half-square triangle units. Draw a diagonal line along the long edge of the template. Rotate the template to the opposite corner of the unit and draw a second line as shown.

5. Place a 4½" x 5½" dark rectangle right sides together with each pieced rectangle. Stitch on each of the drawn lines; cut between the lines, creating 2 blocks as shown below.

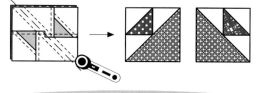

Quilt Top Assembly

BLOCK SET	
Crib	8 x 12
Lap	10 x 16
Twin	14 x 20
Twin	18 x 22

1. Arrange the blocks in the required number of rows for the quilt size you are making. Refer to the "Block Setting Options" on page 81 or design your own setting.
2. Sew blocks together in rows, pressing seams in opposite directions from row to row. Sew rows together.

BORDERS

BORDER STRIPS		
	Inner Border 1½" wide	Outer Border 3½" wide
Crib	5	5
Lap	6	7
Twin	7	8
Queen	8	9

Refer to "Borders" on pages 102–3 for cutting and measuring directions.
1. Cut the required number of inner and outer border strips and join as needed to make borders long enough for your quilt.
2. Measure the quilt top and cut borders.
3. Pin and sew borders to the quilt, adding the side borders first and then the top and bottom borders.

Quilt Finishing

Refer to the general finishing directions on pages 101–4.
1. Layer the quilt with batting and backing; baste.
2. Quilt as desired.
3. Bind the edges.

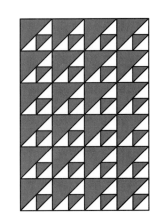

Block Setting Options

Fish

Use the versatile Mary's Triangles technique to make this whimsical fish quilt. Color photos: page 28.

FINISHED SIZE:

Crib 43½" x 51"

Lap 51" x 72¾"

Twin 65½" x 94½"

Queen 87¼" x 101¾"

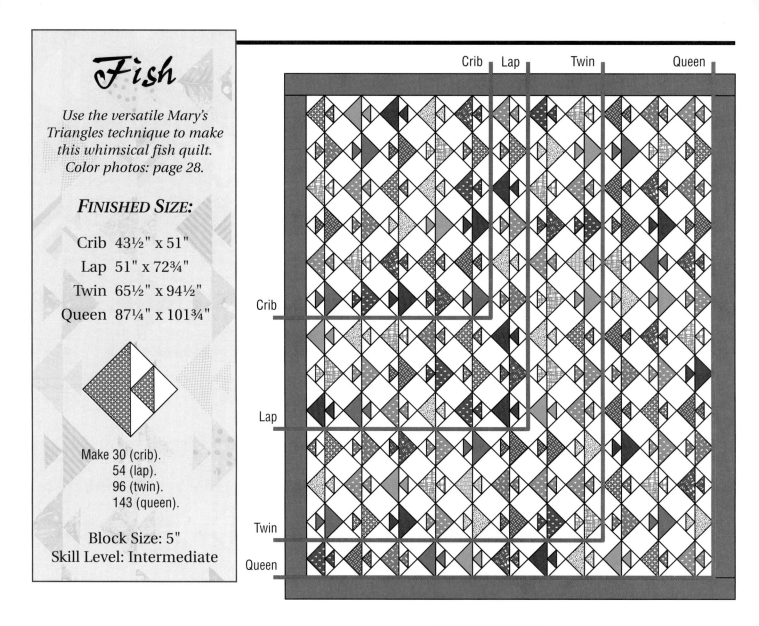

Make 30 (crib).
54 (lap).
96 (twin).
143 (queen).

Block Size: 5"
Skill Level: Intermediate

	CRIB	LAP	TWIN	QUEEN
Fabric: *44" wide*				
9" x 22" Pieces* (in fish colors)	8	14	24	36
Background	2 yds.	2¾ yds.	4½ yds.	6⅛ yds.
Border	½ yd.	¾ yd.	1 yd.	1¼ yds.
Backing	2¾ yds	3½ yds.	6 yds.	7¾ yds.
Batting	46" x 53"	59" x 75"	75" x 99"	91" x 107"
Binding	½ yd.	⅝ yd.	⅝ yd.	¾ yd.

*One piece makes 4 fish.

Cutting

For all quilt sizes:
From each fish fabric, cut 2 pieces, each 5½" x 6½", for the bodies and 2 squares, each 3⅜" x 3⅜", for the tails.

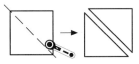

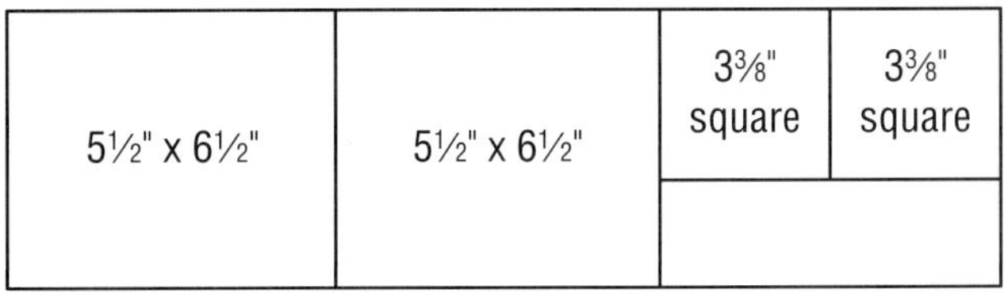

	FIRST CUT		SECOND CUT	
	# Strips	Strip Width	# Pieces	Dimensions
Crib Background	2	3⅜"	15	3⅜" x 3⅜"
	3	4"	30	3" x 4"
	4	5½"	22*	5½" x 5½"
	2	10"	5**	10" x 10"
Lap Background	3	3⅜"	27	3⅜" x 3⅜"
	4	4"	54	3" x 4"
	6	5½"	42*	5½" x 5½"
	2	10"	7**	10" x 10"
Twin Background	5	3⅜"	48	3⅜" x 3⅜"
	8	4"	96	3" x 4"
	12	5½"	79*	5½" x 5½"
	3	10"	9**	10" x 10"
Queen Background	7	3⅜"	72	3⅜" x 3⅜"
	11	4"	144	3" x 4"
	18	5½"	122*	5½" x 5½"
	3	10"	11**	10" x 10"

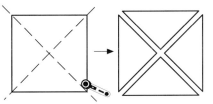

Reserve 2 squares. Cut these once diagonally for 4 corner setting triangles.

**Cut squares twice diagonally for side setting triangles.*

Block Assembly

1. Place one 3⅜" x 3⅜" background square right sides together with one 3⅜" x 3⅜" fish-colored square. Draw a line diagonally from corner to corner. Stitch ¼" from each side of the line.

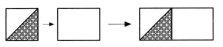

2. Cut on the line. Press the half-square triangle units toward the darker side. Repeat with remaining squares.

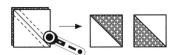

3. Sew the background 3" x 4" rectangles to the half-square triangles.

4. Sew pairs of these units together, making sure that both half-square triangle units in each completed unit are the same fabric.

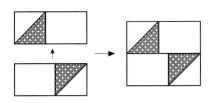

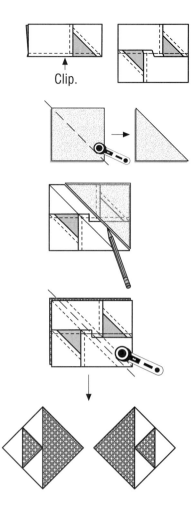

Clip.

5. Clip the seam allowance to the seam line in the center so that you can press the seam away from the squares in opposite directions.

6. Cut a 5½" square of template material, then cut the square in half diagonally.

7. Place the template on the wrong side of the pieced unit, with the corner of the template matching the outer corner of each square. Draw a diagonal line along the long edge of the template. Rotate the template to the opposite corner of the unit and draw a second line as shown.

8. Place a 5½" x 6½" rectangle of matching fish fabric right sides together with each pieced rectangle. Stitch on each of the drawn lines. Cut between them, creating 2 fish as shown at left.

Quilt Top Assembly

1. Arrange Fish blocks and 5½" background squares, following the quilt plan on page 82. Remember to reverse the direction in which the fish are "swimming" for each horizontal row.
2. Sew blocks together in diagonal rows. (See "Diagonal Settings" on pages 101–102.)
3. Sew a side setting triangle of background fabric to each row end.
4. Sew the rows together.
5. Sew a corner setting triangle to each corner of the quilt.

BORDERS

Refer to "Borders" on pages 102–3 for cutting and measuring directions.
1. Cut the required number of 4"-wide border strips and join as needed to make borders long enough for your quilt.
2. Measure the quilt top and cut borders.
3. Pin and sew borders to the quilt, adding the side borders first and then the top and bottom borders.

BORDER STRIPS

Crib	4
Lap	6
Twin	8
Queen	9

Quilt Finishing

Refer to the general finishing directions on pages 101–4.
1. Layer the quilt with batting and backing; baste.
2. Quilt as desired.
3. Bind the edges.

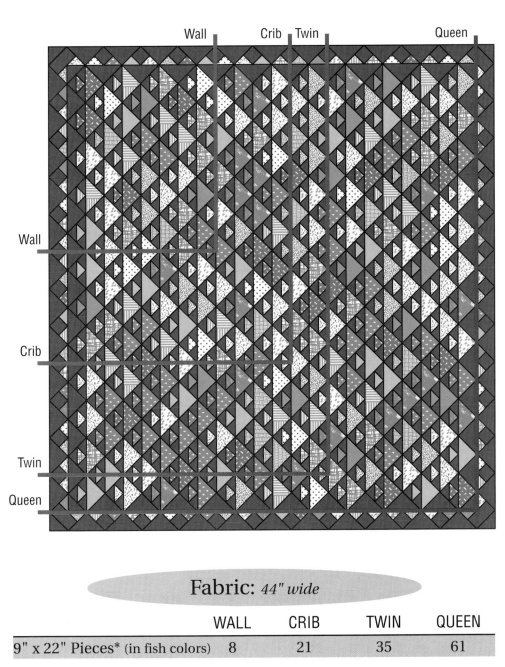

Wall   Crib   Twin   Queen

Wall

Crib

Twin

Queen

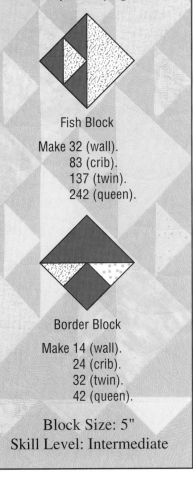

After Dark

This quilt is made using the same Mary's Triangles blocks as the Fish quilt on page 82. Set close together, the Fish blocks give a "school of fish" appearance. Refer to the fabric requirements and cutting directions given for the Trees quilt, omitting the tree trunk fabric. (Use the same fabric for the fish's tail and body.) Follow directions for making the Trees quilt on page 87, except set the Fish blocks so the large triangles point to the side instead of pointing up. Color photo: page 28.

Fish Block

Make 32 (wall).
83 (crib).
137 (twin).
242 (queen).

Border Block

Make 14 (wall).
24 (crib).
32 (twin).
42 (queen).

Block Size: 5"
Skill Level: Intermediate

Fabric: *44" wide*

	WALL	CRIB	TWIN	QUEEN
9" x 22" Pieces* (in fish colors)	8	21	35	61

One piece makes 4 fish.

See the Trees quilt "Fabric" chart on page 88 for remaining yardage requirements.

Cutting

1. From each of the 9" x 22" pieces (fat eighths) of fish fabric, cut the following pieces. Cut a 3" x 3" corner block square from only 8 of the 9" x 22" pieces. See the cutting layout below.

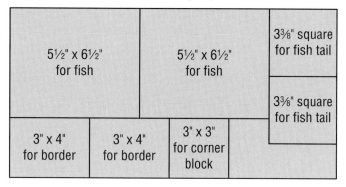

BACKGROUND FABRIC

	# 3⅜" Strips	# Squares
Wall	2	16
Crib	4	42
Twin	6	69
Queen	11	122

2. Referring to the chart at left, cut the number of 3⅜" squares of background fabric required for your quilt size.
3. Cut additional background fabric pieces as directed in the cutting chart for the Trees quilt on pages 88–89, substituting the 3⅜" squares from the cutting layout above for half-square triangle "trunks."

Block Assembly

1. Following steps 1–8 of the directions on pages 83–84 for Fish block construction, make the number of Fish blocks required for the quilt size you are making. Refer to the cutting layout above for Fish blocks.
2. Make border and corner blocks. (See "Border and Corner Blocks" on pages 90–91 of the Trees quilt.)

Quilt Top Assembly

1. Arrange the Fish blocks and Mary's Triangles border blocks as shown in the Trees quilt plan on page 87, rotating the Fish blocks 90° so that the triangles point to the side.
2. Follow directions on page 91 for finishing the Trees quilt.

Wall

Crib

Twin

Queen

Trees

When the Mary's Triangles units are turned so the large triangle points up, the resulting pattern looks like trees. By adding Mary's Triangles blocks around the edges of the quilt, a pieced border is "built in" to the quilt. This method of adding pieced borders is shown in detail in my book Painless Borders. Color photos: page 29.

FINISHED SIZE:

Wall	42" x 35"
Crib	49" x 63"
Twin	56" x 84"
Queen	84" x 91"

Tree Block

Make 32 (wall).
83 (crib).
137 (twin).
242 (queen).

Border Block

Make 14 (wall).
24 (crib).
32 (twin).
42 (queen).

Block Size: 5"
Skill Level: Intermediate

Fabric: *44" wide*

Note:

The crib quilt size is oriented horizontally; all other sizes are oriented vertically.

	WALL	CRIB	TWIN	QUEEN
9" x 22" Pieces (in tree colors)	8	21	35	61
Tree Trunks	⅓ yd.	⅝ yd.	¾ yd.	1¼ yds.
Background	2 yds.	2¾ yds.	4 yds.	6 yds.
Inner Border	⅜ yd.	½ yd.	½ yd.	⅝ yd.
Outer Border	¾ yd.	⅞ yd.	1¼ yds.	1⅜ yds.
Backing	1⅜ yds.	3 yds.	5 yds.	7½ yds.
Batting	39" x 46"	53" x 67"	60" x 88"	88" x 95"
Binding	⅜ yd.	½ yd.	⅝ yd.	¾ yd.

Cutting

1. From each of the 9" x 22" pieces (fat eighths) of tree fabric, cut the pieces, following the cutting layout below. You will have fabric remaining for scraps. Cut a 3" x 3" corner-block square from only 8 of the 9" x 22" pieces.

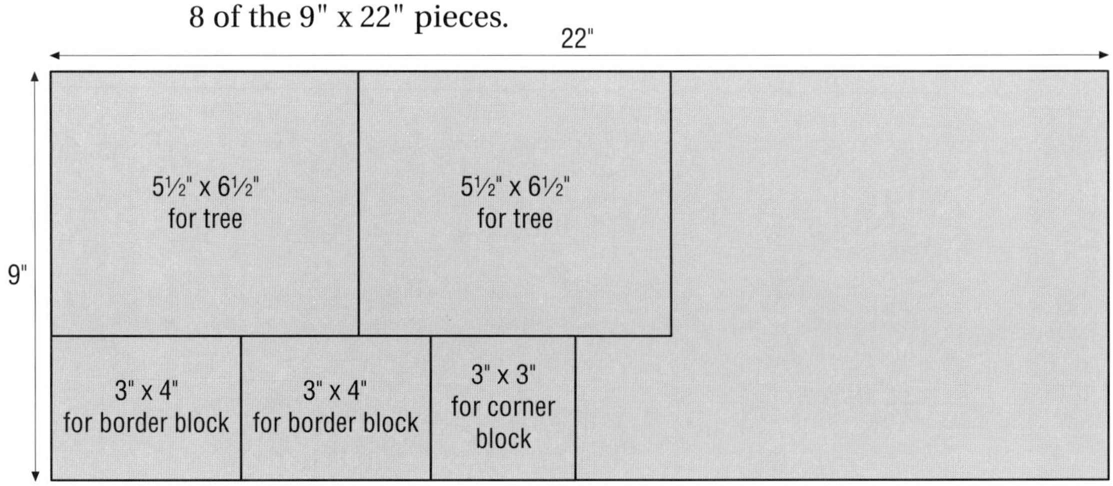
22"
9"
5½" x 6½"
for tree
5½" x 6½"
for tree
3" x 4"
for border block
3" x 4"
for border block
3" x 3"
for corner
block

2. Choose the cutting chart for the quilt size you are making. From background fabric, cut the following pieces:

| | FIRST CUT | | SECOND CUT | |
	# Strips	Strip Width	# Pieces	Dimensions
Wall				
Tree Blocks	3	4"	32	3" x 4"
Borders	2	3"	14	3" x 3"
	2	5½"	8	3" x 5½"
			2*	5½" x 5½"
			7	5½" x 6½"
	2	10"	5**	10" x 10"
Crib				
Tree Blocks	6	4"	83	3" x 4"
Borders	2	3"	24	3" x 3"
	3	5½"	8	3" x 5½"
			2*	5½" x 5½"
			12	5½" x 6½"
	2	10"	7**	10" x 10"
Twin				
Tree Blocks	10	4"	137	3" x 4"
Borders	3	3"	32	3" x 3"
	4	5½"	8	3" x 5½"
			2*	5½" x 5½"
			16	5½" x 6½"
	3	10"	9**	10" x 10"
Queen				
Tree Blocks	18	4"	242	3" x 4"
Borders	3	3"	42	3" x 3"
	5	5½"	8	3" x 5½"
			2*	5½" x 5½"
			21	5½" x 6½"
	3	10"	12**	10" x 10"

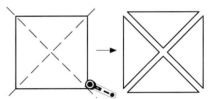

*Cut squares once diagonally for 4 corner setting triangles.

**Cut squares twice diagonally to make side setting triangles.

Block Assembly

1. Following directions for making half-square triangle units on pages 14–15, construct grids using background and tree trunk fabrics. Draw the grid squares 3⅜" to make 3" cut (2½" finished) half-square triangle units. (One grid yields 24 units.)

3" x 3" cut
Make 32 (wall).
83 (crib).
137 (twin).
242 (queen).

NUMBER OF GRIDS	
Wall	1½
Crib	3½
Twin	6
Queen	10½

2. Sew 3" x 4" rectangles of background fabric to half-square triangle "tree trunks."

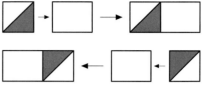

3. Sew pairs of these units together as shown.

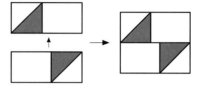

4. Sew Mary's Triangles blocks as required for the quilt size you are making. Follow the directions given on page 84 for the Fish blocks, steps 5–8, substituting tree fabrics for fish.

Note:

Use tree colors at random; each 3" x 4" rectangle used to make the Mary's Triangle unit should be a different color.

Border and Corner Blocks

1. Sew one 3" x 3" background square to a 3" x 4" tree-colored rectangle, right sides together.

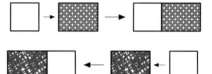

2. Sew pairs of these units together as shown.

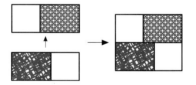

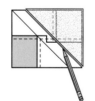

3. Place the same 5½" triangle template that you used to make the Tree blocks on the wrong side of the pieced unit, with the corner of the template matching the outer corner of the square. Draw a diagonal line along the long edge of the template. Rotate the template to the opposite corner of the unit and draw a second line as shown.

4. Place a 5½" x 6½" background rectangle with each pieced rectangle, right sides together. Stitch on each of the drawn lines. Cut between them, creating 2 border blocks. Make the number of blocks for your quilt size, referring to the block diagram on page 87.

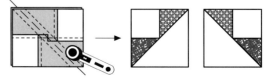

5. For corner blocks, sew 3" tree-colored squares to each end of 4 of the 3" x 5½" rectangles of background fabric, using the folded corner technique. (See "Folded Corners," page 13.) Press seam allowances toward the triangle.

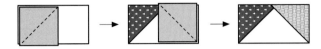

6. Sew the remaining 3" x 5½" background rectangles to the pieced rectangles as shown. Press seam allowances toward the triangles.

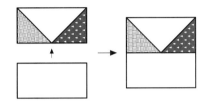

Quilt Top Assembly

1. Arrange the Tree blocks and Mary's Triangles border blocks as shown in the quilt plan.
2. Sew blocks together in diagonal rows. (See "Diagonal Settings," pages 101–2.) Press seam allowances in opposite directions from block to block.
3. Sew a setting triangle of background fabric to the ends of each row. Press.

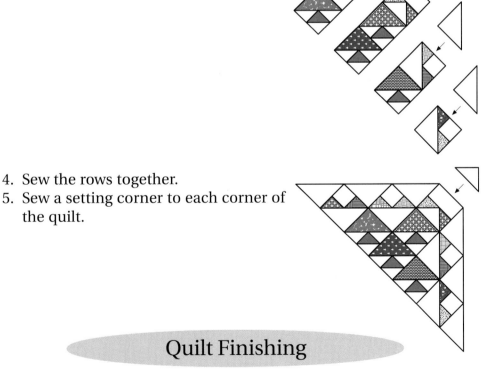

4. Sew the rows together.
5. Sew a setting corner to each corner of the quilt.

Quilt Finishing

Refer to the general finishing directions on pages 101–4.
1. Layer the quilt with batting and backing; baste.
2. Quilt as desired.
3. Bind the edges.

Pinwheel Star

The Pinwheel Star pattern is an adaptation of a traditional design pictured in the book 1001 Patchwork Designs *by Maggie Malone. Using the Mary's Triangles construction technique makes it fast and easy. Color photo: page 25.*

FINISHED SIZE:

Twin 55" x 75"
Double 75" x 95"
King 95" x 115"

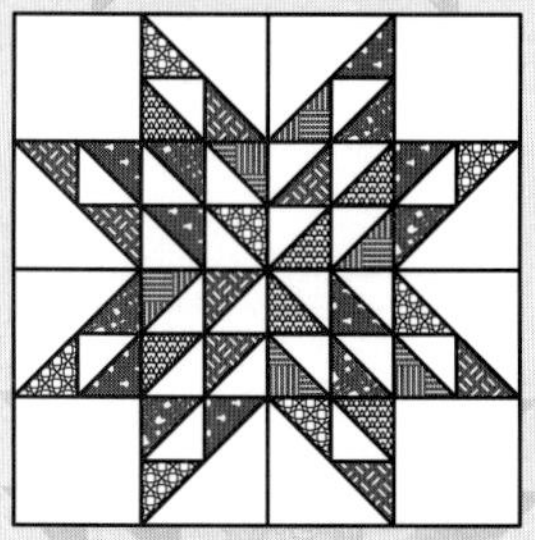

Make 6 (twin).
12 (double).
20 (king).

Block Size: 16"
Skill Level: Intermediate

Note:

Choose 2½" cut (2" finished) half-square triangle units from your prepared pieces to replace light and dark fabric requirements. (See "Scrap Preparation," page 8.)

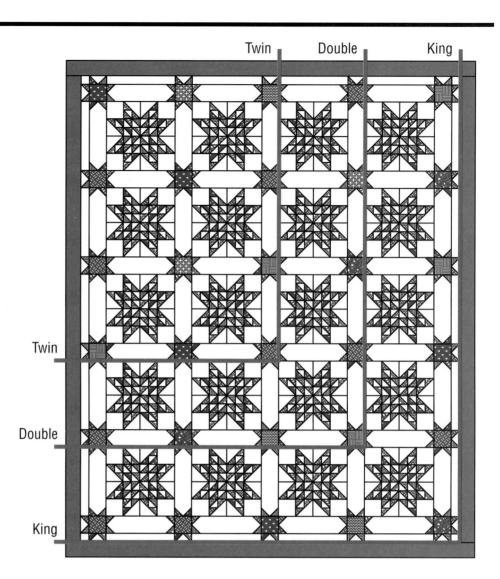

Fabric: *44" wide*			
	TWIN	DOUBLE	KING
9" x 22" Light Pieces	6	12	20
9" x 22" Dark Pieces	6	12	20
Dark Fabric (for Mary's Triangles)	½ yd.	¾ yd.	1¼ yds.
Background	3 yds.	4¾ yds.	7 yds.
Various Dark Fabrics (total for setting stars)	¾ yd.	1¼ yds.	1¾ yds.
Border	1¼ yds.	1¾ yds.	2 yds.
Backing	3½ yds.	6 yds.	8½ yds.
Batting	59" x 79"	79" x 99"	99" x 119"
Binding	½ yd.	¾ yd.	¾ yd.

Cutting

Fabric	# Strips	Strip Width	# Pieces	Dimensions
	FIRST CUT		**SECOND CUT**	

Twin

Fabric	# Strips	Strip Width	# Pieces	Dimensions
Dark Fabric (for Mary's Triangles)	4	2½"	48	2½" x 3½"
Background	3	5½"	24	4½"x 5½"
	4	4½"	24	4½" x 4½"
			14	4½" x 2½"
	3	16½"	17	4½" x 16½"
			10	2½" x 16½"
	1	2½"	4	2½" x 2½"
Setting Stars **Dark Fabrics**	2	4½"	12	4½" x 4½"
	6	2½"	96	2½" x 2½"

Double

Fabric	# Strips	Strip Width	# Pieces	Dimensions
Dark Fabric (for Mary's Triangles)	8	2½"	96	2½" x 3½"
Background	6	5½"	48	4½" x 5½"
	7	4½"	48	4½" x 4½"
			18	4½" x 2½"
	5	16½"	31	4½" x 16½"
			14	2½" x 16½"
	1	2½"	4	2½" x 2½"
Setting Stars **Dark Fabrics**	3	4½"	20	4½" x 4½"
	10	2½"	160	2½" x 2½"

King

Fabric	# Strips	Strip Width	# Pieces	Dimensions
Dark Fabric (for Mary's Triangles)	14	2½"	160	2½" x 3½"
Background	9	5½"	80	4½" x 5½"
	11	4½"	80	4½" x 4½"
			22	4½" x 2½"
	7	16½"	49	4½" x 16½"
			18	2½" x 16½"
	1	2½"	4	2½" x 2½"
Setting Stars **Dark Fabrics**	4	4½"	30	4½" x 4½"
	15	2½"	240	2½" x 2½"

Make 144 (twin).
288 (double).
480 (king).

2½" x 2½" cut

NUMBER OF GRIDS	
Twin	6
Double	12
King	20

1. From the 9" x 22" pieces of dark and light fabrics, make the required number of 2½" cut (2" finished) half-square triangle units for the quilt size you are making. If you use the grid method, draw 2⅞" grid squares. Press seam allowances toward the darker fabric.

2. Stitch 2½" x 3½" dark rectangles to half-square triangle units as shown in the diagram below. Press toward the dark side.

Make 48 (twin).
96 (double).
160 (king).

3. Sew pairs of units together as shown below.

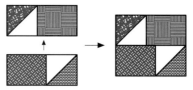

4. Clip the seam allowance to the seam line in the center so that you can press the seam away from the squares in opposite directions as shown. Press.

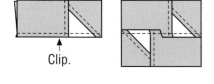

Clip.

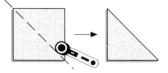

5. Cut a 4½" square of template material, then cut the square in half diagonally.

6. Place the template on the wrong side of each pieced unit. Match the template corner to the outer corner of one of the half-square triangle units. Draw a diagonal line along the long edge of the template. Rotate the template to the opposite corner of the unit and draw a second line as shown.

7. Place a 4½" x 5½" background rectangle with each pieced rectangle, right sides together. Stitch on each of the drawn lines. Cut between them, creating 2 Mary's Triangles units as shown below. Press toward the dark side.

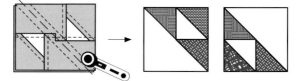

8. Sew the remaining half-square triangles together in groups of 4 as shown at left. Press.

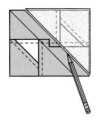

9. Using the Mary's Triangles units, the half-square triangle units, and the 4½" background squares, assemble the blocks, following the diagram below. Sew the units into horizontal rows; sew rows together. Press the seams in opposite directions from row to row.

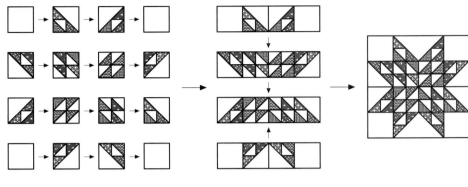

SASHING STRIPS

1. Using the folded-corner technique on page 13, place a 2½" dark square, right sides together, on opposite corners of each 4½" x 16½" sashing strip as shown below. Stitch. Sew a 2½" dark square to each remaining corner of the sashing rectangle as shown. Press seam allowances toward the dark.

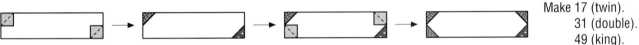

Make 17 (twin).
31 (double).
49 (king).

2. Join blocks and 4½" x 16½" sashing strips in horizontal rows, beginning and ending each row with a sashing strip.

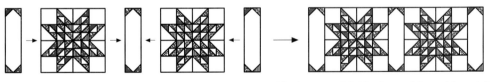

Assemble 3 rows of 2 blocks and 3 sashing strips (twin).
4 rows of 3 blocks and 4 sashing strips (double).
5 rows of 4 blocks and 5 sashing strips (king).

3. Sew a 2½" x 16½" vertical sashing rectangle to each end of the row. Press. (See quilt plan on page 92.)

4. Sew a 4½" dark square to one end of each 4½" x 16½" horizontal sashing rectangle. Press toward the dark square.

Make 8 (twin).
15 (double).
24 (king).

5. Join rectangles to make horizontal sashing rows as shown. Add one 4½" dark square to the end as shown. Press.

Assemble 4 rows of 2 sashing units (twin).
5 rows of 3 sashing units (double).
6 rows of 4 sashing units (king).

6. Sew a 2½" dark square to each end of a 2½" x 4½" sashing rectangle to make a folded-corner unit. Press toward the triangle.

Make 14 (twin).
18 (double).
22 (king).

7. Sew one 2½" x 4½" folded-corner rectangle to each end of the horizontal sashing row as shown. Press toward the dark square.

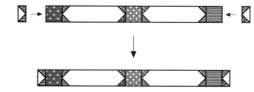

8. Sew one 2½" x 4½" folded-corner rectangle to the end of a 2½" x 16½" sashing rectangle. Press.

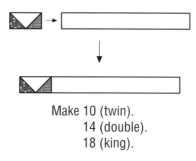

Make 10 (twin).
14 (double).
18 (king).

9. Sew these sashing rectangles together to make a 2½"-wide sashing strip for the top and bottom of the quilt. Add one 2½" x 4½" folded-corner unit to the end as shown. Press. Add a 2½" sashing square at each end. Press.

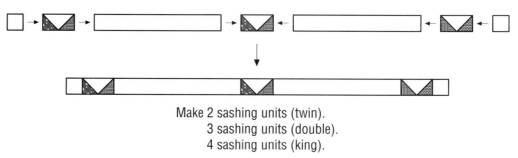

Make 2 sashing units (twin).
3 sashing units (double).
4 sashing units (king).

10. Referring to the diagram below, sew rows of blocks and 4½"-wide sashing strips together, matching seams between each block. Press seam allowances toward sashing strips. Sew a 2½"-wide sashing strip to the top and bottom of the quilt, positioning the strip so the triangles point away from the center. Press.

BORDERS

Refer to "Borders" on pages 102–3 for cutting and measuring directions.
1. Cut the required number of 3½"-wide border strips and join as needed to make borders long enough for your quilt.
2. Measure the quilt top and cut borders.
3. Pin and sew borders to the quilt, adding the side borders first and then the top and bottom borders.

BORDER STRIPS	
Twin	7
Double	9
King	10

Quilt Finishing

Refer to the general finishing directions on pages 101–4.
1. Layer the quilt with batting and backing; baste.
2. Quilt as desired.
3. Bind the edges.

Ocean Waves

Traditionally, the most challenging part of making the Ocean Waves block is fitting the half-square triangle units around the center square. Dividing the center square in quarters using the Mary's Triangles technique simplifies construction of that section of the block. Color photo: page 30.

FINISHED SIZE:

Crib 51" x 71"

Twin 71" x 91"

Double 91" x 111"

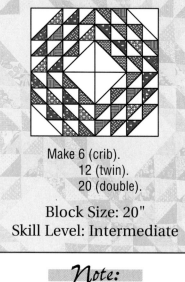

Make 6 (crib).
12 (twin).
20 (double).

Block Size: 20"
Skill Level: Intermediate

Note:

You may choose 3" cut (2½" finished) half-square triangle units from your prepared pieces to replace the assorted light and dark fabrics. (See "Scrap Preparation," page 8.) For the number of half-square triangle units required, see step 1 of "Block Assembly."

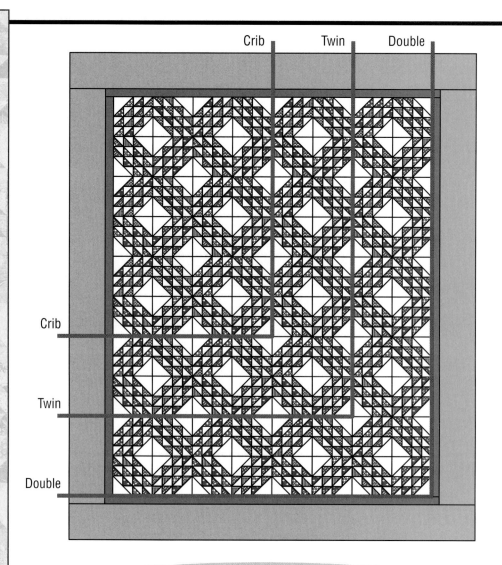

Fabric: *44" wide*

	CRIB	TWIN	DOUBLE
Assorted Dark Fabrics (total)	1⅜ yds.	2¼ yds.	3¾ yds.
Assorted Light Fabrics (total)	1⅜ yds.	2¼ yds.	3¾ yds.
Assorted 3" x 4" Dark Rectangles	24	48	80
Assorted 3" x 4" Light Rectangles	24	48	80
Background	⅞ yd.	1½ yds.	2½ yds.
Inner Border	½ yd.	⅝ yd.	¾ yd.
Outer Border	1 yd.	1¼ yds.	1½ yds.
Backing	3¼ yds.	5½ yds.	8¼ yds.
Batting	56" x 76"	76" x 96"	96" x 116"
Binding	½ yd.	⅝ yd.	¾ yd.

Cutting

Fabric	FIRST CUT # Strips	FIRST CUT Strip Width	SECOND CUT # Pieces	SECOND CUT Dimensions
Crib Background	4	5½"	24	5½" x 6½"
Twin Background	8	5½"	48	5½" x 6½"
Double Background	14	5½"	80	5½" x 6½"

Block Assembly

Make 240 (crib).
480 (twin).
800 (double).

3" x 3" cut

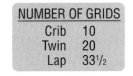

NUMBER OF GRIDS
Crib   10
Twin   20
Lap   33½

1. From the assorted light and dark fabrics, make the required number of 3" cut (2½" finished) half-square triangle units for the quilt size you are making. If you use the grid method, draw 3⅜" squares onto the grid. Press seam allowances toward dark fabric.

2. Sew 1 half-square triangle unit to each light and dark 3" x 4" rectangle. Repeat for the number required for the quilt size you are making. Press seam allowances toward the triangle.

Make 24 (crib).
48 (twin).
80 (double).

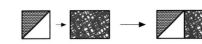

Make 24 (crib).
48 (twin).
80 (double).

3. Sew pairs of these units together as shown, keeping light rectangles with light rectangles and dark rectangles with dark rectangles.

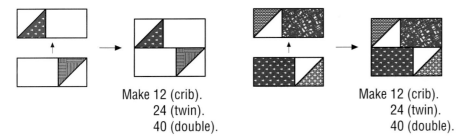

Make 12 (crib).
24 (twin).
40 (double).

Make 12 (crib).
24 (twin).
40 (double).

4. Clip the seam allowance to the seam line in the center so that you can press the seam away from the squares in opposite directions as shown. Press.

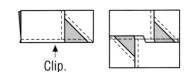

Clip.

5. Cut a 5½" square of template material, then cut the square in half diagonally.

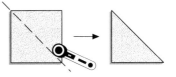

6. Place the template on the wrong side of each pieced unit. Match the template corner to the outer corner of one of the half-square triangle units. Draw a diagonal line along the long edge of the template. Rotate the template to the opposite corner of the unit and draw a second line as shown.

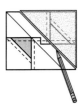

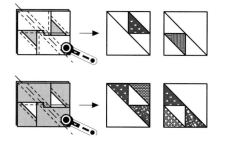

7. Place a 5½" x 6½" background rectangle with each pieced light and dark rectangle, right sides together. Stitch on each of the drawn lines and cut between them, creating 2 Mary's Triangles units as shown at left. Press.

8. Following the diagrams at right, sew the remaining half-square triangle units together in pairs, then sew the pairs together into groups of 4.

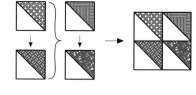

9. Sew 2 sets of half-square triangle units and 2 sets of Mary's Triangles units together into quarter blocks as shown. Press.

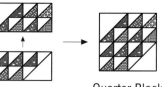

Quarter Block

10. Sew 4 quarter blocks together, carefully noting placement of dark and light triangles. Press.

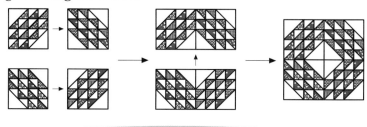

Quilt Top Assembly

1. Arrange the blocks into the required number of rows for the quilt size you are making.
2. Sew blocks together in rows, pressing seams in opposite directions from row to row. Sew the rows together. Refer to the quilt plan on page 98.

BORDERS

Refer to "Borders" on pages 102–3 for cutting and measuring directions.

1. Cut the required number of inner and outer border strips and join as needed to make borders long enough for your quilt.
2. Measure the quilt top and cut borders.
3. Pin and sew borders to the quilt, adding the side borders first and then the top and bottom borders.

BORDER STRIPS

	Inner Border 2" wide	Outer Border 4½" wide
Crib	6	6
Twin	8	8
Double	10	10

Quilt Finishing

Refer to the general finishing directions on pages 101–4.

1. Layer the quilt with batting and backing; baste.
2. Quilt as desired.
3. Bind the edges.

Quilt Assembly and Finishing

Diagonal Settings

Sewing the blocks of a quilt together on the diagonal is no more difficult than sewing them in a straight setting, but there are some tricks to make them easier to handle.

SIDE SETTING TRIANGLES

Setting blocks on the diagonal creates triangular-shaped areas on the edges and at the corners that must be filled, either with pieced triangles (partial blocks) or with plain triangles called side setting triangles. Pieced or plain, side setting triangles must have the straight grain of the fabric on the longest edge of the triangle. This helps keep the outer edges from stretching, making it easier to attach borders or binding.

For plain side setting triangles:
1. Measure the diagonal of your completed block.

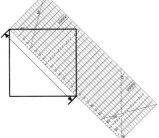

2. Add 2" to that measurement.
3. Use this new measurement to cut squares of the chosen fabric.
4. Cut the squares twice diagonally, to yield 4 triangles.

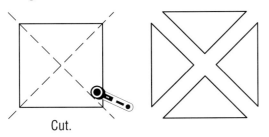

Cut.

These triangles are much larger than necessary for your quilt, but because sewing places stress on bias edges, the outside edges tend to curve inward. Therefore, if you cut triangles exactly the right size and they shrink inward, they might end up being too small. It is easy to trim off the edge but impossible to add more to it!

Place these edge triangles in the spaces at the edge of your quilt and piece them to the ends of the blocks as you sew the rows together, following the diagram below.

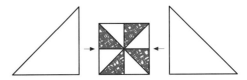

Notice that the right-angle points of the triangles are kept on the same line as the block edges, and the sharper points of the triangles are allowed to overhang the block. This is essential to keep the long edge straight. To trim the triangle points off, lay your cutting ruler's edge across the top of the blocks even with the raw edge of the block and cut.

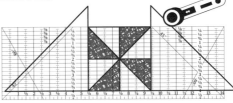

CORNER SETTING TRIANGLES

Cut corner setting triangles from squares cut the same size as your pieced squares. Then cut these squares in half on the diagonal to yield two triangles. For each quilt, cut two of these squares to yield four triangles, one for each corner.

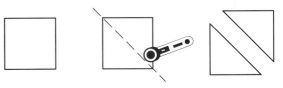

101

To assemble a diagonally set quilt:

1. Lay out the blocks and corner and side setting triangles in diagonal rows.
2. Sew the blocks together in diagonal rows.
3. Trim the side setting triangle points as shown on page 101.
4. Sew the rows together, adding the two corner setting triangles last as shown.

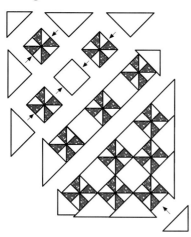

5. After completing the quilt top, check to see that opposite sides of the quilt are equal in length. Carefully fold the top in half lengthwise, matching seam intersections on opposite sides. If the sides are not the same length, resew the diagonal seams that join rows together on the longer side, taking a slightly deeper seam allowance. Just an extra ⅛"-wide seam on each row will add up to 1" when four rows are adjusted in this manner.

   Repeat this step, folding the quilt in half crosswise to measure the top and bottom of the quilt; adjust as needed.

6. Square up the quilt and trim the outer edges, leaving a ¼"-wide seam allowance as shown below.

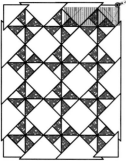

Note:

Until a diagonally set quilt is layered and basted for quilting (page 103), it is extremely important to use care when handling it. The vertical and horizontal planes of these quilts are on the bias and will stretch very easily. While basting, pat the quilt flat rather than trying to push the fullness to one edge or the other. Be careful that you do not stretch or distort the fold lines when you fold the unbasted and unquilted top. You may stretch the center of the quilt to the point where it will never lie flat again!

Borders

I prefer to cut border strips across the width of the fabric and join them end to end, as needed. Less fabric is required when borders are cut this way.

To keep your quilt square, it is important to cut the border strips to fit before you add them to the quilt top. The quilts in this book have borders with straight-cut corners or borders with cornerstones.

BORDERS WITH STRAIGHT-CUT CORNERS

1. To measure the quilt top for borders, lay two border strips along the center of the quilt top, lengthwise. Trim the ends even with the raw edges of the quilt. Fold border strips in half and then in quarters and mark the folds with pins. Mark both long sides of the quilt in the same manner.

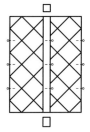

2. Pin borders to the sides of the quilt, matching the markings. Pin about every 3" along the border, easing if necessary. Stitch borders to the quilt.

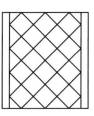

3. Repeat this procedure for the top and bottom borders.

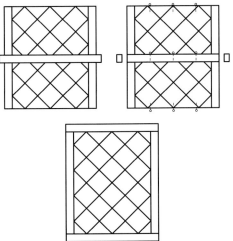

BORDERS WITH CORNER SQUARES

1. If your borders have corner squares, measure and cut the strips for all four sides before sewing any borders to the quilt.

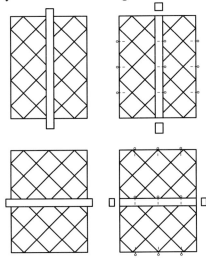

2. Pin and stitch the side borders to the quilt top as directed for straight-cut borders.

3. Sew a corner square to each end of the top and bottom borders, then attach them to the quilt.

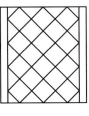

Layering and Basting the Quilt

Many publications include information about basting and quilting quilts, whether by hand or machine. Marsha McCloskey's *Lessons in Machine Piecing*, or Trudie Hughes's *Template-Free™ Quiltmaking* have very good directions for these techniques. I have not included them here because of their wide availability elsewhere.

Quilt Backing

Although some directions for quilt backings specify running seams lengthwise and placing them away from the center of the quilt, this often requires more fabric than necessary. Instead, I prefer to calculate the yardage required for quilt backs, allowing the least amount of excess fabric. (Notice that I do not use the word "waste." All excess fabric from the back of my quilts becomes strips, half-square triangles, or pieces for the front of other quilts. Nothing is wasted!)

For all quilts up to 75" long, piece the backing with one crosswise seam in the center. Measure the width of the quilt, add 6", and double this number for the amount of fabric you will need to purchase (in inches). Divide by 36" to calculate yards.

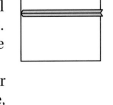

For quilts that are longer than 75" and up to 75" wide, piece the backing with one lengthwise seam in the center. Measure the length of the quilt, add 6", and double this number for the amount of fabric you will need to purchase (in inches). Divide by 36" to calculate yards.

Piece backings for quilts larger than 75" x 75" (up to 110" x 110") with three lengths of fabric. Measure the shortest side and add 6". Triple this measurement for the amount of fabric you will need to purchase (in inches). Divide by 36" to calculate yards.

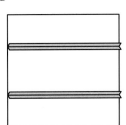

Binding

1. Cut straight-grain, 2½"-wide binding strips across the full width of the fabric. Use the guide below to find the amount of fabric required for straight-grain binding for standard-size quilts:

Quilt Size	Yardage
Crib	⅜ yd.
Lap	½ yd.
Twin	⅝ yd.
Full or Queen	¾ yd.
King	1 yd.

2. Sew the strips together to make one long strip and press seam allowances open. Press the strip in half lengthwise, wrong sides together.

3. Open out the strip at one end and fold over the corner to form a 45° angle as shown.

4. Beginning about 6" away from one corner, pin the binding to the quilt top, keeping binding raw edge even with the quilt top raw edge. End at the next corner.

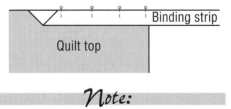

Note:

Wait until binding has been attached before trimming away excess backing and batting.

5. Miter the corner by folding the binding strip away from the quilt, creating a 45° fold at the corner of the quilt as shown.

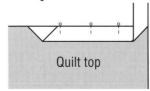

6. Fold the binding strip back on itself, parallel with the next edge of the quilt.

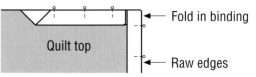

7. Pin the miter and continue pinning the raw edges to the next corner. Repeat the steps above for each corner.

8. Where the ends of the binding meet, open out the folded edge and place the end of the binding inside the fold. Refold the binding, enclosing its end.

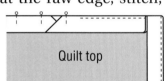

9. Stitch the binding with a ⅜"-wide seam allowance to within 1½" from the corner. Remove the pin at the miter, fold the miter toward you, and stitch to a point within ⅜" from the edge. Backtack.

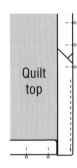

10. Remove the quilt from the sewing machine and refold the miter back over the previous stitching. Beginning at the raw edge, stitch, continuing along the next side of the quilt until you reach the corner.

11. Repeat for each corner. End by stitching through all thicknesses where the two ends of the binding meet.

12. Trim the edge of the quilt backing and batting about ¼" beyond the raw edge of the quilt top. Fold the binding over, tucking in the extra ¼" of batting and backing along the raw edge to make a firmly filled binding. Hand stitch on the wrong side, mitering each corner as shown below.

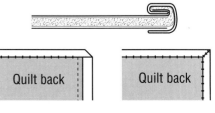